THE FUTURE OF FASHION

THE FUTURE OF FASHION

UNDERSTANDING SUSTAINABILITY IN THE FASHION INDUSTRY

TYLER LITTLE

NEW DEGREE PRESS

COPYRIGHT © 2018 TYLER LITTLE

THE FUTURE OF FASHION

Understanding Sustainability in the Fashion Industry

ISBN   978-1-64137-140-7   *Paperback*

978-1-64137-141-4   *Ebook*

To my parents.

CONTENTS

STOP #4

INTRODUCTION

LET'S TAKE A TRIP

———

I want to take you on a trip.

Now you are probably thinking, "What does that mean?" Well, let me explain.

I want to be your guide on a journey through the world of sustainable fashion. Over the last six months, I have talked to entrepreneurs in this space and employees at some of the most sustainable fashion companies in the world. I have also read countless articles and reports on the state of the industry. Now that I have made the journey, I feel confident I can steer you in the right direction.

The trip I'll be taking you on will be a lot smoother than the one I experienced. My voyage was like a road trip where you have an idea of where you want to end up, but you have no idea how to get there and just have to take it as it comes. You might spend a few hours heading in the wrong direction and have to turn completely around. Or you may think you are lost and suddenly realize you are actually right where you need to be. The point is, my journey was all over the place. But now that I've made the trip, please allow me to be your guide on your own expedition of learning and discovery.

The next logical question is—well, where are we going? We are about to embark on an adventure through the sustainable fashion space. The easiest way to break it down is to view it as having four major stops we want to make along the way.

Stop #1: Industry Analysis

On our first stop, we will look at the sustainable fashion space from a high level. We need to first have a general idea of the industry to help contextualize some of the information we will learn later.

Stop #2: Why We Need Change

The next stop can be a bit emotional. We will look at why we need to see change within the fashion Industry. In this section, you'll hear some stories from people I was lucky enough to encounter on my journey. These stories can be heartwarming, heart wrenching, and inspiring—sometimes all three at the same time.

Stop #3: How Change Can Happen

After we understand the necessity for change, we will look at how this change is currently happening in the industry and how it can continue. We will explore exciting topics like innovation, psychology, and what roles celebrities play.

Stop #4: Change Is Possible

This stop, the final stop in our journey, can be particularly satisfying and inspiring because we can look at why change is a possibility. We will delve into both general ideas and specific examples of companies to support this change being possible.

But we will not just explore the possibility of change. We will do a deep dive into some companies that are nearly perfect examples of what it means to be sustainable.

I am excited for us to reach our destination, but we cannot jump ahead of ourselves. We need to make sure and take the time to explore all of our stops before we arrive.

I want to warn you this trip can be a little intense at times. Like any good road trip, it will have its ups and downs. However, our final destination makes it all worth it.

* * *

Right now there is a revolutionary movement occurring in the fashion industry to establish more sustainable practices that will reduce the environmental footprint of the industry and help ensure it is making a positive impact on the millions of communities that are affected by it.

Currently the fashion industry is performing abysmally in terms of sustainability. It is extremely resource intensive and not only utilizes a great deal of fixed resources, but also results in a great deal of pollution of our air and water. In 2015 the fashion industry consumed 79 billion cubic meters of water, emitted 1,715 million tons of CO_2, and produced 92 million tons of waste. These figures can be difficult to conceptualize, so here are some other ways to think about them. That 79 billion cubic meters of water is enough to fill 32 million Olympic-sized swimming pools, and the CO_2 emissions is like 230 million passenger cars driving around for a year. For waste creation just think about this fact. In a year the world population creates 1.6 times more waste than what the earth can absorb in the same time frame.

If all of these metrics are not concerning enough, consider the fact that by 2030 the global population is expected to reach

8.5 billion people. For perspective, the current world population is roughly 7.5 billion people. We are already consuming natural resources at a faster rate than the earth can replenish them, and an extra billion people will only cause the severity of this issue to grow.

Clearly, we have a serious issue that needs to be addressed. As someone with a passion for both fashion and the environment, I decided I wanted to take on the task of writing an unbiased review of the industry.

I have always been interested in the fashion industry, but when I say fashion I don't mean luxury fashion like Gucci, Prada, and Versace—a conclusion people often jump to rather quickly. When I say I'm interested in fashion, I mean I like clothes, footwear, accessories, etc. as a form of self-expression. I love how you can put together different combinations of clothing to represent yourself in so many different ways. I think the way you present yourself is an opportunity to represent who you are. Even if you don't care about what your clothes look like, this is a choice and form of self-expression in itself.

Once I fully realized my passion for the fashion industry, I wanted to learn more; upon further research I found some troubling things that tarnished my initial impression. It only takes a few Google searches to realize that the fashion industry is doing some serious damage both in terms of environmental and societal issues. This realization of just how polluting and corrupt the industry can be was disheartening. Then, I discovered sustainable fashion.

Once I discovered the world of sustainable fashion, I was hooked. The sustainable fashion space is dynamic, innovative, and revolutionary. It is dynamic and innovative because it has to be. While sustainability is important, it cannot be expected that companies will be sustainable because it is the "right" thing to do.

In order for sustainability to become part of business operations, the practice must improve a company's efficiencies and provide some sort of monetary incentive. At first glance, this may seem like a pessimistic way to view business, but I don't think of it like that. If you want socially minded companies to thrive in the marketplace, it is only logical that you need to make sustainability a profitable endeavor. In order for a brand to be successful in the long term, they need to be able to remain profitable over the long term.

The sustainable fashion space is revolutionary because it is attempting to enact systematic change in one of the largest industries in the world. The global apparel market is valued at over three trillion dollars and affects people all over the world. In order to create lasting change, the industry needs to embrace emerging technologies and innovations.

So why should you read this book and not another one about sustainable fashion? Consider this. I am a twenty-two-year-old college kid with no experience in the industry.

Yup, you read that right. I think my lack of experience in the industry is actually my biggest strength. Because I have no ties to a company, no ties to an organization, no ulterior motives, really just no reason to write anything but the truth, you can trust that I am presenting you with an unbiased report on the fashion industry and what role sustainable fashion can play within the industry.

This book is really intended for anyone who wants to learn about the sustainable fashion space in an easily digestible manner. Instead of just viewing it as sustainability, thing about this—do you like innovation? psychology? inspiring stories? socially minded business? fashion? If you answered yes to any of these, this book has something for you.

After reading this book, you will walk away with a knowledge of what is really happening in the fashion industry—something not many people can say. Often, we can become absorbed in our everyday lives and forget about what is going on around us. This book serves as a means for people to become informed about a wildly important topic.

STOP #1

INDUSTRY ANALYSIS

Before embarking on any journey, it is important to give yourself a solid understanding of where you want to explore. You would not take off on a cross-country road trip without doing your due diligence. Understanding the fashion industry is similar in this respect.

For us this means familiarizing ourselves with the current state of affairs in the fashion industry. Looking at the industry broadly first will help us contextualize what we learn in our coming stops.

In these next couple of chapters, you can expect to not only gain an understanding of where the fashion industry stands today, but also what kind of effects the industry will have on the environment if it continues to do business in the same manner it has in the past.

This stop is largely centered around something called the Pulse Report—a comprehensive view of the state of the fashion industry, which I found to be one of the most useful compilations of information I came across. For me discovering the Pulse Report was like a sports fanatic suddenly discovering ESPN. It has information you would otherwise have to scour the internet to find on your own, and everything has already been vetted for accuracy.

Besides the Pulse Report, we will also take a look at some of the main factors driving change in the industry—both on the business side and consumer side of things.

Well that's enough preparing you for our journey. Let's get going!

CHAPTER 1

THE PULSE REPORT

Taking a broad and holistic look at the fashion world is important as it can help us gain insight into where the industry is heading and get a clear idea of opportunities for growth within the space. In a report created through the collaboration of the Boston Consulting Group (BCG) and the Global Fashion Agenda (GFA), we find this necessary assessment of the industry.

The Global Fashion Agenda is a nonprofit with the mission of prompting the fashion industry to change the way we produce and consume fashion with consideration for our long-term future. Being a nonprofit helps give more validity to the work they do since they are not trying to change the fashion industry based on their own company's motives.

In this chapter I will look at the first half of the report that BCG and GFA put together. First, I will provide some summary of the facts and statistics about the current size of the industry and some projections for its growth by the year 2030. Next, we will look at what impact the fashion industry's growth will have if it continues conducting business under the current model (based on the projected growth by 2030). Then we will look at the main tool created for the assessment of industry sustainability, the Pulse Score. Finally, we will move to some of the findings from the utilization of the Pulse Score including an analysis of the different environmental and social impacts of each stage of the product creation process.

In terms of revenue and employment, the fashion industry is one of the largest industries in the world. In 2016 the apparel and footwear market generated over 1.8 billion dollars in revenue and employed over 60 million people. An industry of such colossal size clearly impacts not only those working in it and consuming its products, but everyone around the world. The industry's effect can be felt outside of people directly involved because of the negative influence business operations have on the environment.

With the global population expected to reach 8.5 billion by 2030, the market will continue to expand rapidly. This increasing population results in an expected apparel consumption increase of 63.5 percent from 62 million tons per year to 102 million tons per year.

To get an idea of the environmental costs, BCG and GFA put a monetary value on all of the externalities from this rapid growth. In terms of environmental impact, water consumption will increase by 50 percent, energy emissions will increase by 63 percent, and waste created will jump from 92 million tons to 148 million tons.

When looking at the societal impact of the industry, we see areas of great concern as well. Workers paid less than 120 percent of minimum wage will increase 52 percent from 14 million to 21 million, and the number of recorded injuries in apparel production will jump from 1.4 million to 1.6 million.

With such a wide reach in terms of people influenced and the inevitability of rapid growth, the need for change only becomes increasingly imperative. Although the fashion industry is not the only problem, it is clearly a major contributor with its current linear model that results in a great deal of waste and usage of natural resources.

The overuse of resources like water and energy will result in rising prices as the goods become more scarce. This coupled with rising labor costs could result in an earnings before interest and taxes (EBIT) margin decline of 3 percent if brands do not adapt and change their practices. A decline of this amount means a profit reduction of $52 billion per year for the industry as a whole. Overall, bad for the planet and bad for business.

In order to provide the fashion industry with more transparency and a meaningful standard to measure its sustainability performance, BCG and GFA created the Pulse Score. This score is developed from data and information from two main resources. The first is the Higg Index, a "self-assessment tool" developed by the Sustainable Apparel Coalition that large brands use to measure the environmental and social impacts of their supply chains. BCG and GFA took this data and combined it with a survey of industry executives—the Pulse Survey—and interviews with experts to validate their conclusions and processes.

These factors all combine to create the Pulse Score. However, while the Higg Index is useful, it is only intended for larger companies. The Pulse Score alleviates this specificity because it provides a standard means of measurement that extends to all players in the industry—from small local companies to large global brands. The Pulse Score's creation allows for transparency within the fashion industry.

As stated in the report, "it gives the industry a common understanding of what the most critical issues across the value chain and by impact areas are. Perhaps more important, it creates a foundation for the landscape for change, channeling investment and innovation into those areas that smart businesses will capture and benefit from." Additionally, because BCG and GFA, moving forward from this initial release, intend to create the report annually, the industry will be able to assess its improvements or lack thereof over the coming years.

The Pulse Score measures sustainability on a scale from 0 to 100. It is designed so that a score of 100 is unattainable because it represents a perfect company with no negative impact. Scores over 70 are considered very strong, scores between 60-69 are strong, scores in the 30s and below are considered weak.

This detailed analysis found that the fashion industry performs very poorly with an overall Pulse Score of 32. However, this poor performance was not universal across the space. Research found that sustainability performance was generally linked to company size rather than price positioning.

In general, the largest brands along with some niche sustainability-focused smaller players are doing very well in terms of their impact. While small and midsized companies (which account for half of the industry) scored the lowest. Companies in the top revenue quartile have a Pulse Score of 63 while ones in the bottom quartile have a score of just 11.

This is not that surprising because larger companies have far more resources they can dedicate to sustainability practices and more power over suppliers to demand certain standards. Smaller companies lack these resources and the ability to control what happens in their supply chain, so even when they have good intentions they are often unable to follow through.

This analysis led to a great deal of unique findings that should be considerations for all brands, manufacturers, retailers, and consumers around the world. Speaking in geographic terms, the report found that European brands scored higher on environmental dimensions. Conversely, US brands achieved higher scores in dimensions related to social and labor practices.

The report looked at eight major areas of impact across both environmental and societal issues. The environmental impact areas included water, energy, waste, and chemicals. The societal impact areas were labor practices, health and safety, community engagement, and unethical practices.

One particularly interesting finding is that fashion brands were much more likely to score higher in areas like health and safety and chemical usage. The explanation for the higher scores in health and safety is linked with the level of media attention issues like these receive. When statistics come out about exposure to hazardous materials for employees in factories or when reports arise about a factory collapse, such as the one in Bangladesh that killed two hundred people, the media takes note and therefore consumers are much more aware of these issues.

Companies are more motivated to ensure the health and safety of their workers so they do not have these major public relations issues. Public relations scandals damage companies' reputations, cause outrage among consumers, and often have serious negative consequences on profits.

The higher scores in chemical impact are due to regulation. The European Union's REACH (Registration, Evaluation, Authorization and restriction of Chemicals) regulation limits the chemical pollution that brands can have. The lessened negative impacts in these areas show that consumer action and regulation can be powerful tools in enforcing responsible and ethical business practices.

The Pulse Score report provides detailed analysis of each step of the product creation process, assigning scores to each step from design and development all the way to end of use. Next we will take a look at each of these stages and some of the findings from BCG and GFA.

When looking at the design and development phase, fashion brands must overcome two challenges. The first is that many of these fashion brands lack awareness of the social and environmental impact of their products. Without this awareness, they do not factor their impact into the process of designing the products. This is extremely problematic because this unawareness at the initial planning stage can cause many irreversible issues as you move farther down the supply chain. The second is brands tend to use the design phase as an opportunity to cut costs. When product teams design apparel or footwear, they are guided by how to make the product for as cheaply as possible without consideration for the external social and environmental costs of product creation.

The next step of the process is the raw materials stage. This stage is one of the most important stages of the process because of the dramatic effect it has on the potential recyclability of products. Some of the worst and most commonly used materials in the fashion industry are leather and natural fibers like cotton, wool, and silk.

Cotton, for example, requires the use of harmful chemicals, accounting for the consumption of 4 percent of nitrogen fertilizers and phosphorous globally (not to mention the extreme usage of water in its production). While the raw materials stage has the second lowest score along the value chain, a terrible 17, there is a serious gap between the top and bottom performers.

Large companies as well as niche sustainability-focused small players achieve scores as high as 60 while smaller companies score as low as 5. Clearly, alternative materials are in existence, but have not yet gained the necessary popularity within the industry.

In the report BCG and GFA add that for this stage to see improvements "both the technology and economics of recycling need to improve dramatically, ideally with a single standard to help with scaling up to commercialization." This type of improvement will come from investments in innovation and industry-wide collaboration.

Following the raw materials stage is the processing stage, which includes all actions taken to prepare the fabrics for use, such as dyeing, weaving, and spinning. Overall, this stage scored the second highest Pulse Score for the industry with a 38. However, there was a tremendous amount of variation between brands with scores ranging from 80 to 0.

A more in-depth look at this variation indicates great room for improvement with smaller companies. Larger brands generally do a more effective job at minimizing their impact here.

Chemical usage is one of the main issues to be addressed in this stage of the process, posing both environmental and social concerns. In terms of environmental impact, the harmful chemicals used in both dyeing and treating fabrics pollute the earth and use significant amounts of water in the process. In terms of societal concerns, many workers in the supply chain are being exposed to these chemicals in large volume on a daily basis and are at risk for serious long-term health effects.

After processing we move on to the manufacturing stage where labor, health, and safety are the primary concerns. Consumers are starting to demand more transparency in this area and are expressing a great deal of concern for the impact the assembly of their clothes may have on the lives of workers. This increasing concern from consumers has resulted in brands not only adhering to labor standards set through regulation, but actually taking it upon themselves to closely monitor their suppliers and demand certain standards.

This stage serves as an example that consumers hold a great deal of power and can incite change within the industry as well. One sector of the fashion industry that is seeing exceptional success in this part of the process is sports apparel with a very impressive Pulse Score of 76.

From manufacturing we move to the transportation stage of the process, which includes both packaging and distribution. Transportation achieves the highest Pulse Score of 41. This higher score is due to the fact that the transportation needs of fashion are very similar to those of other industries. As a result, the fashion industry can capitalize on the strategy and innovations other industries have made regarding transportation.

Even the lowest performers at this stage do not fall below 28 while the best brands score as high as 90. Additionally, this is one of the few cases where we see cost and environmental impact closely tied together because high costs of air shipments discourage companies from utilizing it as a means of transporting their products.

The retail stage comes after transportation and has a Pulse Score of 28. There is not much variation in this figure across the industry with the exceptions of luxury brands and sustainability champions. Luxury brands often score as low as 13 while sustainability-focused companies score as high as 75.

Regulation will not play a part in reducing environmental impact as many brands will try to limit energy use—things like lighting and air conditioning—as a cost-saving measure. This stage presents great opportunity for brands as it is the main point of contact with customers. At this stage brands have the greatest opportunity to try and influence consumer behavior.

As we move past the retail stage, we get into the final two stages—consumer use and end of use. These stages are a little different because at this point the products are in the hands of consumers, and the impact of the fashion industry is dependent upon their actions. However, this is not to say that fashion brands cannot do their part in improving the environmental impacts of this stage.

The consumer use stage includes how a consumer handles, repairs, and washes their garments and footwear. The industry scores low on consumer use with a 23, though it is necessary to note that it is difficult to gain a full assessment of this stage because of the lack of the comprehensive data.

One of the issue we see here is the changing behavior and mindset of consumers toward their apparel. With the popularization of fast fashion, the number of garments purchased by a consumer has doubled over the last decade. Additionally, it is possible that many brands do not view this stage as their responsibility and do not devote resources to try and influence consumer behavior.

However, this is not true of all brands as some work to promote awareness through their marketing efforts. This type of messaging can also be beneficial for a company because it promotes more engagement between customers and the brand. Another trend that helps to reduce impact at this stage is the emergence of clothing rental services. Clothing rental services help to prolong the life of products by providing consumers with a means for a one-time use of products.

The final stage of the process is end of use, where the life cycle of a product comes to an end. When a consumer has finished with a product, it can be passed on to a new consumer, upcycled, downcycled, full recycled or disposed of as waste.

Unfortunately, by far the most common outcome for a garment when it reaches its end is the disposal of it as waste where it then ends up in landfills. This fact results in the end of use stage receiving the lowest score across all the stages with just a 9 for the industry. Similar to the consumer use stage, the low score here is affected by the lack of responsibility brands feel for it.

Additionally, in interviews with representatives across the industry, the Pulse Report found that brands consider pursuing recycling options as one of the least relevant ways for them to improve their sustainability platforms. For the fashion industry to see improvement in this stage, a shift in mindset on both the parts of consumers and brands must occur. Fashion brands can help to expedite this process by not only starting to take more responsibility for their products once they leave the store, but also by committing resources to help spread awareness to change consumer behavior.

Phew that was a lot of information, right? I hope you aren't suffering from information overload too much. (I know at times I was when reading the report.) I thought about simplifying this opening chapter more but decided against it because having a solid understanding of this industry is imperative for our journey. Plus, I knew you could handle it.

It is important for us to take a look at each and every stage of a garment's life cycle because it can help us to better understand some of the topics we will explore in later chapters.

Just for a quick recap, the stages of a product life cycle were as follows: design and development, raw materials, processing, manufacturing, transportation, retail, consumer use, and end of use. By understanding these stages, you can contextualize some of the information we will learn in coming chapters.

Now you can think, "Oh, so that innovation helps for the design stage," or, "That company is focused on improving the sustainability of their retail," and so on.

By taking an in-depth look at the fashion industry and how sustainable it is at each step of the product creation process, we can more easily find potential opportunities for improvement and innovation.

CHAPTER 2

DRIVERS OF THE SUSTAINABLE FASHION MOVEMENT

———

Research on the fashion industry, conducted at the Kelley School of Business, shows that some macro-level trends are fueling the surge of the sustainable fashion industry. Some of the key trends discussed in the study are the growth of the circular economy, increased demand for Corporate Social Responsibility (CSR) practices, increased consumer awareness, the birth of the sharing economy, and technological innovation.

The idea of a circular economy is about focusing on how we can take products and materials already in existence and use them to create products of greater value. This trend separates economic growth and the use of finite resources. A circular economy consists of both upcycling and recycling.

Upcycling is taking resources that would normally be discarded and using them to create something of greater value. For example, Rareform is a company that takes billboards and turns them into things like backpacks. Upcycling is not just a trend we see in the fashion industry—this is something happening in a variety of industries. A good example is the countless DIY home renovation ideas you can find online.

Recycling, as you probably know, is converting materials from old products into new ones. An example of recycling in the fashion industry is a company like Matt & Nat, who recycle water bottles to create the inside lining of their luxury handbags.

Both the processes of upcycling and recycling give new value to products that would otherwise become waste. The popularizing of these ideas in both the fashion industry and beyond is a key driver to the sustainability movement.

Another driver in the sustainable fashion movement is the increased prevalence of Corporate Social Responsibility (CSR) statements by brands. Often for global brands their actual manufacturing processes are outsourced to foreign nations with lower labor costs. This outsourcing separates the production process from the design and marketing operations of the business. This often results in terrible practices such as unsafe working conditions, child labor, and workers not being paid livable wages.

To avoid involvement in these practices many brands are committing to things like sweatshop-free labor and joining the World Fair Trade Organization. Additionally, there has been a greater push for locally sourced products. Locally sourced products try to minimize the distance between where a product is produced and where it is consumed. All these things are becoming key considerations in brands' formulation of CSR policies.

Another trend, and perhaps one of the strongest drivers of the sustainable fashion push, is increased consumer awareness. Consumers have grown increasingly aware of the negative impact fashion can have. This has resulted in a change in consumer preferences regarding consumption.

Besides the increase in consumer demand for green products, consumers are also changing the way they view ownership of products, which will be covered in the sharing economy chapter. Previously consumers viewed owning their clothes, shoes, and accessories as essential, but the rapidly growing sharing economy shows this idea is becoming a thing of the past.

Additionally, a change in the consumer mindset of younger generations has helped to drive sustainable fashion. Research shows that younger generations value experiences (like a trip to a foreign country or seeing their favorite band live) more than previous generations. This increasing value placed on experience results in younger consumers spending less on material things—like clothing. This change has forced the fashion industry to innovate and find new ways to add value so they may remain both relevant and profitable.

The sharing economy is centered on the idea of collaborative consumption. This new way of consuming products is best described as "the expansion and reinvention of exchanging, swapping, bartering, sharing, loaning, and donating practices, usually between people not previously connected." The growth of the sharing economy can be seen in the growth of the apparel rental industry as companies like Rent the Runway continue to see great success. Collaborative consumption provides a new avenue for innovation and an alternative way for consumers to spend their money.

A final driver in the sustainable fashion movement is technological innovation. Technological innovation is occurring along all dimensions of the supply chain. The industry has seen a boom of new and more sustainable materials being discovered and utilized in textile production. Additionally, new systems are being created to improve supply chain efficiency, resulting in things like the reduction of waste, decrease of pollution, and reduction of water and energy usage in production.

An interesting area of innovation gaining increased traction is wearable tech. The wearable tech field is working to create wearables that can monitor the wear and tear of products to aid in determining when and how apparel should be discarded.

In this chapter, we discussed some of the major trends we see pushing the sustainable fashion movement forward. The continued growth and popularization of these trends will help to move the entire fashion industry toward increased sustainability.

STOP #2

WHY WE NEED CHANGE

You made it to stop number two! Now that we have covered some of the initial background information, we can start to dive a little deeper into other topics this book will explore.

In the last chapter, I introduced the idea of why we need change, but in the coming chapters I will absolutely convince you of this fact.

At this stop you will hear some firsthand accounts from people involved in the fashion industry, an explanation of why change is not only necessary for the fashion industry from a moral standpoint but also for long-term survival, and a distressing account of an industry tragedy.

CHAPTER 3

REVELATION

Have you ever witnessed something you'll never forget? Read a statistic or story that just doesn't leave your head?

In many of my interviews with leaders in the sustainable fashion space, they could point to a specific moment in time when they had this type of experience. Once they realized how negative the impact of some common practices in fashion are, they could not just turn a blind eye.

Moments like these can change your life.

The impact fast fashion has on the environment and the abuses of labor within the industry are often occurring unknowingly to most consumers. With so many different factors affecting the buying decision process, consumers are already overloaded with information. Often considerations of how their apparel was made and what ramifications that process may have do not cross a consumer's mind.

However, once consumers become aware of facts like the fashion industry being one of the most polluting industries in the world, producing thirteen billion tons of waste each year, it is difficult to forget. The following are some stories of people involved in the fashion industry who experienced such a revelation. Once they were made fully aware of the negative impact fast fashion can have, they not only changed their purchasing habits but set out to make a difference through their business ventures.

One inspiring story of revelation and action that I had the privilege of hearing comes from a conversation I had with the founder of Futurewear, Alejandra Carrero. Alejandra initially started a company whose aim was to empower women by selling trendy clothing at a reasonable price so that all women had the opportunity to dress how they wanted, regardless of their socioeconomic status.

However, one trip to China in 2011 changed her perspective on her entire business. She visited one of the factories she was purchasing from and was appalled by what she saw. She not only witnessed terrible working conditions, but also child labor. As she walked around the factory, she saw young girls whom she guessed ranged in age from eight to fourteen years old.

These girls were too frightened to make eye contact with Alejandra as she toured the facility. Alejandra speaks a bit of Mandarin and even tried to talk to some of the workers but was shooed away because they did not want to risk being disciplined later for speaking.

After this visit, Alejandra was beside herself; she had been trying to make a difference in the lives of women in the United States and did not even realize what was going on abroad in order for her to accomplish this goal. She knew she had to do something about this. With a new sense of purpose and inspiration, she created another company, Futurewear. The commitment she felt to her new cause was so strong that she returned to school to pursue an MBA at Babson College so she could gain the necessary knowledge and skills to embark on her new initiative of founding Futurewear.

Futurewear is an online database of brands that Alejandra and her team has vetted to ensure they have ethical and sustainable practices. This database empowers consumers with the information they need to make informed purchasing decisions and support brands that align with their values. This model not only helps consumers, but it also helps brands by promoting the ones that are trying to do business in an ethical way. Without her trip to China and incredible passion and drive, Futurewear would have never been created.

Another inspiring story of revelation I encountered on my journey through the sustainable fashion space came from my conversation with Meagan Cann, founder of the Workspace Collective. After college Meagan worked for a major department store and was exposed to some of the horrors of the industry.

In her time here, she witnessed the power major department stores have over the factories that supply for them. Because these department stores purchase in such large quantities from these factories, they have the power to drive prices down to ridiculously low margins. While this works out well for the department stores, it has terrible ramifications for the workers in these factories.

As prices are driven lower and lower, the wages of the factory workers are cut to allow the factories to keep running. These wage cuts impede the workers' abilities to provide their families with basic human needs like food. Upon realization of what was occurring, Meagan decided she could no longer take part in this and left her job at the department store.

After leaving her job, Meagan returned to school at the Fashion Institute of Technology to study sustainable design. After her time at FIT she decided to start her own company to make a difference—the Workspace Collective. This company helps promote sustainability by building a community around the movement. Located in Danbury, Connecticut, Meagan brings together local designers who are producing their garments in sustainable ways.

These stories are not meant to be tragic accounts of some of the atrocities occurring in the fashion industry, but rather serve as inspiration for how one person can set out to make an impact and contribute to the growing trend of sustainability and ethics in the fashion industry.

CHAPTER 4

A CONVINCING ARGUMENT FOR CHANGE

———

Fashion, like any other industry, is a business. Therefore, they have to consider the company's ability to be profitable in the present and make the best decisions for the firm's future success.

Sustainability is a major consideration for both of these things, but in this story, I will focus on companies' needs to address the future of their operations. The threats posed by environmental change are inevitable and growing greater as time passes. With environmental change happening so quickly, companies no longer have a choice of whether they want to consider sustainability in their operations.

Considerations for environmental impact have become necessities when companies assess the future of their operations. Patagonia founder Yvon Chouinard really drives home this point with his words, "Who are businesses really responsible to? Their customers? Shareholders? Employees? We would argue that it's none of the above. Fundamentally, businesses are responsible to their resource base. Without a healthy environment there are no shareholders, no employees, no customers and no business." With this thought in mind, we will now look below to see some of the major threats companies will be facing in the future.

One of the most pressing threats facing the industry is the cost of raw materials. The fashion industry depends on various natural resources that are finite in their volume. Companies need to take a step back and look at alternative materials to use in their production because the earth cannot keep pace with our current rate of consumption.

One of the most concerning resources being overutilized by the industry is fresh water. The fashion industry is notorious for its excessive use of water in the production processes. For example, according to the World Wildlife Fund, over 5000 gallons of water are used just to make a t-shirt and pair of jeans. In a report conducted by McKinsey & Company, they predicted that at our current rate of water consumption we will outstrip our supply by 40 percent in the year 2030.

Another threat the fashion industry faces because of environmental change is disruption of its labor force. A well-known fact is the majority of fashion brands outsource their labor production to foreign countries. As climate change continues to cause sea levels to rise, many countries are put at risk. The Organisation for Economic Co-operation and Development (OECD) found that four of the five countries most affected by these rising sea levels are key players in apparel manufacturing. These countries at risk include China, Vietnam, India, and Bangladesh.

The changing environment is also affecting oil prices, which clearly affect all industries including fashion. Climate change is limiting not only access to oil, but also causing the process of extracting the oil to become more costly. One solution to the volatility of oil prices is for brands to source locally. Local sourcing would not only help cut back on the effects from increasing oil costs, but also help to invigorate local communities.

All these imposing threats revolving around climate change bring another obstacle to the table—regulation. As things like water and oil increase in scarcity, and the damaging effects of the fashion industry are fully felt, regulation will inevitably follow. This regulation will come from governmental organizations; however, the industry could possibly handle the issues itself. If major brands recognize the magnitude of the issue and band together, they can help to counteract some of the negative impacts the fashion industry has had.

One example of uniting to set standards of sustainability is the Sustainable Apparel Coalition (SAC). The Sustainable Apparel Coalition is a collection of brands, retailers, manufacturers, governments, and NGOs (non-governmental organizations) who have banded together to find a universal approach to measuring sustainability performance. Members of the coalition represent each stage of the supply chain, and the revenue of its members totals over five hundred billion dollars. We will dive more into SAC's beginning and its goals in a later chapter.

This chapter serves to show that companies need to consider the environmental impact they are causing, not just for the sake of society as a whole, but also for the long-term future of their company.

CHAPTER 5

CLEARING MISCONCEPTIONS

———

One of the first things I wanted to figure out once I decided to explore and write about the sustainable fashion space was how polluting and damaging is fashion really? I know it's bad, but just how bad is it?

This fact is debated by sustainability experts across the globe, but in reality, it is pretty difficult to take a full assessment of what kind of damage the fashion industry does to the environment. In my own personal search for the answer, I discovered someone else who embarked on this confusing journey—freelance journalist Alden Wicker.

Wicker specializes in sustainable fashion and has had her

work featured in various publications such as *Quartz, Racked, Refinery29, Maxim, Forbes, Huffington Post Green, The Daily Muse*, and mindbodygreen, to name a few. She also started her own leading sustainable lifestyle blog called, EcoCult.

Like me, Wicker had seen the phrase "fashion is the second most polluting industry in the world" pop up in her research over and over. However, in trying to pinpoint where this fact comes from, no credible source confirmed it. Upon a little more digging, I found that this figure actually came from a press release from the Danish Fashion Institute. With even a little more detective work, I found that the press release was eventually pulled because the research the figure was based on was not credible.

Wicker decided to take her research a step further and contacted leaders in the sustainable fashion space to explore this misconception and see if they had a more informative study to reference. She actually received a response from the Danish Fashion Institute. In an email they said, "We don't believe the statement to be accurate either, but we are aware that it has become a popular misconception… We can, however, tell you that fashion is one of the most resource-intensive industries in the world, both in terms of natural resources and human resources." Additionally, she received a response from the Sustainable Apparel Coalition saying that while being the second biggest polluter could be theoretically true, they did not have the metrics to support it.

I wanted to take you on this detour from our road trip to help clarify that, in your own research, you might see this statistic referenced often, but upon further exploration you will likely have no luck discovering its source.

However, I am excited to say that since Wicker originally wrote about her findings in an article published in *Racked* in May 2017, a detailed assessment of industry impact has been taken. That assessment, as you may have guessed, is The Pulse Report, which was the first resource that allowed people to actually begin to get a realistic assessment of the impact fashion has.

In assessing where fashion ranks in terms of pollution compared to other industries, it really depends what metrics you want to look at. So rather than trying to throw a title at the industry, let's just take a look at some statistics collected by the World Resources Institute from various sources that hopefully have the same jaw-dropping effect on you that they had on me.

First, let's talk about the way consumer behavior has been shifting. When we look at consumption in 2014 as compared to 2000, we see that the average consumer purchased 60 percent more clothing but kept each garment for half as long. This trend of increased consumption is a driving factor for poor industry environmental impact as we discussed prior.

How about water consumption in the industry? It takes 700 gallons of water to make one cotton t-shirt. This is enough water for one person to drink for 2.5 years. If that fact is not wild enough for you, just think back to what we mentioned earlier—like the fashion industry using enough water to fill 32 million Olympic-sized swimming pools.

Another consideration is the compounding effect the fashion industry has on the environment. In looking at CO_2 emissions from the 2018 Climate Report, you can see that fashion is the fourth worst polluting industry when using this particular metric. However, the effects of the fashion industry are greater than what they appear when you consider that fashion plays a role in the CO_2 emissions of the three industries performing worse than it in CO_2 emissions. The three industries ranking worse in this metric are electric, agriculture, and road transportation.

Wicker, on her blog, points out some of the connections that the fashion industry has to these three other polluting industries when she writes: "Electricity (often from dirty sources like coal and diesel generators) powers the garment factories. Cotton is an agricultural product. A small portion of clothing's journey is done by road transportation. Polyester is made from plastic, which is a petroleum product. Leather is a byproduct of livestock raised for food."

Throughout the book, we will continue to discuss the impact the fashion industry has on not only the environment but also on social issues. This chapter is meant to clear up some common misconceptions.

CHAPTER 6

FACTORY COLLAPSE IN BANGLADESH

———

April 24, 2013.

This date represents a horrifying day in the fashion industry.

On this date 1,127 workers died when a five-story building, the Rana Plaza, collapsed in Savar, a suburb of the capital of Bangladesh, Dhaka. This was the worst disaster in the history of the garment industry.

One of the most horrifying facts about this tragedy is the obvious neglect that led to this catastrophic situation occurring. One of the first decisions that led to this event was the mayor of the district granting construction approvals for the building that should have never been passed. This led to the addition of an upper floor to the factory that could contain thousands more workers. While this action clearly aligned with the interests of the factory owners, allowing them to see a significant increase in profits, it did not take into account the safety and well-being of those who would be aiding them in the pursuit of profitability.

The addition of this upper flower necessitated the addition of massive power generators to counteract the power outages the top floor would experience since the building was functioning well beyond its intended means. Reports say that the building would literally shake when these generators were turned on each day.

On April 23 the shaking became too much, and the walls of the building began to crack. Workers started to flee the scene as they feared not only for their safety, but for their lives.

Despite many workers pleading to not have to return to work the next morning and an inspection from an engineer that deemed the building unsafe, the workers were told to return to work. The blatant disregard for the safety of these workers continued and the pursuit of productivity was maintained as the top priority.

These workers, fearing for both their lives and their livelihoods, were forced to make a choice between the two. Disobeying the orders would result in losing their only means of providing food for their families, but continuing to work in these conditions would put their lives on the line.

This is a decision no worker should ever be forced to make. Weighing the pros and cons between keeping your job and your life is an absolutely unacceptable position to put workers in. However, these garment workers were forced to make that decision.

What if something like this were to happen again? With Bangladesh being the world's second largest exporter of clothing behind China and supplying for the vast majority of major brands in the marketplace today, this does not seem out of the question unless the fashion industry made some changes. With more than five thousand garment factories in Bangladesh, a large number of buildings are of high concern, so a lot of change is necessary to ensure something like this does not happen again.

Later we will discuss some of the changes to practices and new legislation that resulted from this tragic incident.

STOP #3

HOW CHANGE
CAN HAPPEN

Crazy stuff, huh? While many people have an idea of some of the atrocities occurring in the industry, I think it can be difficult to fully grasp. The last few chapters drove home the point that change needs to occur in this industry.

And that change needs to happen not eventually, but right now.

Now that you are hopefully convinced of the necessity for this change, we will explore how change is already happening and how it can continue to happen.

This next stop is one of the most exciting of our journey. In the coming chapters, we will dive into the question you have been asking yourself—how can change occur in this industry?

A revolution is occurring right now in the fashion industry, thanks to the tireless efforts of dedicated and motivated individuals. Now we will take the time to look at the results of their efforts and see how this revolution is propelling itself forward.

Strap in because this next stop has a lot to take in, but it is a thrilling ride.

CHAPTER 7

COMMUNITY BUILDING

––––

One of the key factors to the sustainable fashion movement succeeding and enacting change is building community—whether that be locally, nationally, or globally.

Community can be built in a variety of ways. You can start an initiative to run events in your area that teach people about how to be more conscious consumers, start a blog, or use a retail store front as a place for people to come and engage with other driven individuals. No matter the scale, resources, or number of individuals associated with your community, every single one of us can make a difference.

One great example of community building at a local level is the work being done by Meagan Cann. She founded the Workspace Collective, a company based in Danbury, Connecticut, that brings together local designers committed to creating sustainable garments. The designers' work is sold in the store, but their involvement does not end there.

When visiting the store, customers can see designers at work and engage with them about their products. This unique setup incites customer curiosity and gets them thinking about how their apparel is created. The designers also engage with customers through workshops led weekly in the store. The content covered ranges from knitting to hand knotted rope bracelets.

The engagement between designers and customers helps create a community around sustainable products. Customer involvement in the store's activities also results in a great deal of word-of-mouth promotion for the Workspace Collective. Most people won't tell their friends about a shirt they purchased at their local mall, but they will definitely tell their friends about an experience as unique as the one they get when they enter the Workspace Collective.

The relationships holding this community together are not just between designers and consumers, but also between the designers themselves. The workspace brings together these talented and driven individuals so they can share their expertise and collaborate.

Another effective way to build community around sustainable

fashion is through online publications like blogs. Tons of these are available to consumers—one example being Kate Black's Magnifeco. Kate Black is a powerhouse within the world of sustainable fashion. She acts as an advisor for the Unite States Environmental Protection Agency, has authored multiple books on the topic, and most relevant to this chapter has helped build the sustainable fashion community through multiple endeavors.

Her blog's main purpose as stated on the site is to be "the digital source for eco-fashion and sustainable living." The blog helps to keep consumers informed about what they can do in their everyday lives to make a difference. One such example is a featured piece called "The Lazy Person's Guide to Saving the Planet." This guide lists things that consumers can change about their everyday habits to help contribute to a more sustainable world.

The blog also helps guide consumers to the brands with the most sustainable and ethical practices. This helps consumers support brands that align with their values and gives additional exposure to brands making a positive impact on the world. But one of the greatest things about creating online publications, like a blog, is providing people with a platform to engage in dialogue about sustainability.

Community building does not need to be limited to just

individuals; it can be on a larger scale through businesses choosing to unite their efforts. Patagonia CEO Rose Marcario said the following: "We're living in a world where business is responsible for more than 60 percent of the pollution of our air and our water and our land, and yet they take very little responsibility. I think what the B Corp community does is it brings together these like-minded companies to be a greater force for good in the world." The whole idea behind the B Corp community is working to redefine what success means in the business world. By banding together with other businesses who are run with a socially minded approach, they can make an even bigger impact together.

Building a community can also be done through event organization. The Global Fashion Exchange (GFX), created by Patrick Duffy, is an excellent example of this. The group runs events all over the world where people can exchange pieces of their wardrobe with one another. This allows people to update their style while also helping to cut back on more garments entering landfills. Clothing is weighed so that the organization can track the overall impact they are having in terms of how much waste has been kept out of landfills.

After weighing, clothes are sorted into high end and streetwear. The number of garments you bring determines how many items you can take from each respective section of the event. Each event also features educational content and inspiring talks from leaders within the industry. So far the GFX has held seven events, in three continents, in four cities.

These efforts have helped them to save over forty thousand pounds of clothing so far. The most exciting part of this is that it is just the beginning. As this event is held in more and more cities around the globe, not only will thousands and thousands of pounds of clothing be saved from landfills, but the conversation about sustainable practices on the part of consumers will continue to pick up steam. Part of making a difference is spreading awareness, and large-scale events like this can do just that.

You know how I mentioned that Kate Black is a legend in the sustainable fashion community? Well, here is another example for you of her community building skills at work. She founded a monthly global event series called EcoSessions, which aims to help connect fashion industry leaders, designers, and citizens to help collaborate and learn about what could be next for the sustainable fashion movement.

When asked where the idea for EcoSessions came from, she said, "I realized the industry needed two things to push it forward: there needed to be more sharing and collaboration between makers, and consumers needed opportunities to hear the stories and see the products. So I created EcoSessions to meet both of these needs. We bring together leaders around a topic or theme (most who have never met) and then ask them to share their stories as a way to activate conscious consumerism."

This idea of community building is key to the sustainability movement. It will help to both spread awareness and bring together driven individuals with a commitment to the cause. The collaboration of these individuals could end up leading to the next big innovation within the sustainability space.

I will close this chapter with a quote from Patagonia CEO Rose Marcario regarding her optimism about our ability to community build. "I would say that I am optimistic because I have seen a few things that I think have really changed the landscape. One is the ability to interconnect in a way that we've never seen before. It's very, very powerful, and we've been funding activists for a long time, so we're very tapped into an activist network. I haven't seen the ability to organize and collaborate in the way that I have seen it today. It is amazing, and it is a wonderful leverage. I think it will really change things. I think that makes me optimistic."

CHAPTER 8

ORGANIZATIONS FOR CHANGE

————

Organizations can be extremely effective, not only for speeding up the rate of change in an industry, but also for helping to ensure that change can have a lasting impact. Consumers can provide the drive and demand for changes, and brands can make the changes happen. But organizations should be put in place to ensure that change is not temporary. Organizations guarantee lasting change through a variety of actions like monitoring and tracking activity within an industry, which empowers companies with the information they need to keep behaving in a responsible way.

Many organizations are taking on this challenge in the sustainability space. Here I will explore some of the most impressive organizations enacting change in the industry and detail the impact they are having.

The Sustainable Apparel Coalition is one of these organizations. Their mission regarding upholding sustainability is twofold— incorporating environmental and social impact. They want to make sure the apparel industry is causing no unnecessary harm to the environment and impacting the communities associated with its activities in the best way possible.

The coalition formed from an unusual partnership between Patagonia and Walmart. The two industry giants came together with the intention of doing the following: "Collect peers and competitors from across the apparel, footwear, and textile sector and, together, develop a universal approach to measuring sustainability performance." To form the coalition, the CEOs of each company wrote a joint letter inviting other global industry leaders to join them in establishing a way to measure the impact their products were having.

Their efforts resulted in the creation of the Higg Index. One of the main tools in the Higg Index is the Materials Sustainability Index, a system that was being utilized by Nike. Nike donated this system to help contribute to the cause. The Higg Index helps encourage transparency within the industry and gives brands a meaningful way to measure their impact and work to reduce it.

The organization has seen great success as their index is now utilized by more than ten thousand manufacturers around the globe. The vice president of sustainability at Levi Strauss & Co, Michael Kobori, had this positive insight into the coalition and the Higg Index. "The Sustainable Apparel Coalition brings brands and vendors together in an equal partnership to drive impact reduction. The Higg Index, which is being used by the majority of our key vendors, helps drive impact reductions in our material issues of water, chemistry, and carbon."

Another organization making waves in the industry is Fair Trade USA. This group advocates for the individuals, families, and communities that are affected by global industries. Their work is crucial because without Fair Trade USA, these individuals would have no way of advocating for their own well-being. The group certifies companies that are doing business in an ethical way, which helps consumers decipher where their money is best spent.

On the company website the first text you see, which is simple yet very powerful, reads: "Every purchase supports something. Fair Trade exists so we can support what's fair." The certification simplifies the buying decision process for socially conscious consumers by providing a seal of approval. The four pillars of their mission are income sustainability, empowerment, individual and community stewardship, and environmental stewardship. The organization aims to help counteract the exploitation of the vulnerable in the pursuit of maximizing profits.

The nonprofit B Lab is a similar organization to Fair Trade USA. They provide a certification for companies that meet their standards of social impact, environmental impact, accountability, and transparency. Their website features some impressive statistics that compare companies they have certified with non-certified companies. For example, B Corp certified organizations are 68 percent more likely to donate at least 10 percent of their profits to charity and 55 percent more likely to cover some portion of their employees' health insurance costs.

The Ethical Fashion Forum empowers brands specifically in the apparel and textile industry to transform their practices with their platform, SOURCE. They use business intelligence and data to enable brands to make changes to their business model. Utilizing these tools, they provide analysis of a brand's operations to help them decipher where and how they can improve their supply chain and practices.

This type of organization is crucial in the success of the sustainable fashion movement because they not only advocate for responsible business within fashion, but they assist brands in making that change. This is a key facet of their organization because often brands may want to make the changes to be more sustainable but do not have the resources or knowledge to do so.

Another group making a difference is the Ellen MacArthur Foundation. This group hopes to accelerate the transitions of business to a circular economy. They work in collaboration with government, business, and academia. Their mission as a thought leader is to discover what is necessary to develop a circular economy and help enable this transition.

Their platform revolves around a variety of aspects. In terms of education, they provide training and learning platforms that help companies build their operations around the idea of a circular economy. They also partner with major companies such as Google, Nike, and Unilever to help discover innovative ways to incorporate a circular economy approach.

Another dimension is providing insight and analysis that helps capture and clearly depict the value of their frameworks. They also help connect various levels of a supply chain to aid in collaboration because this is key to the success of adopting this approach. Finally, they promote their model of a circular economy to a global audience to help bring it more recognition.

One initiative they have that is particularly relevant to the fashion industry is their Circular Fibres Initiative. This initiative acknowledges the size of the fashion industry and how innovation within the textile industry can have a huge impact. They help companies apply their concepts and frameworks within a fashion supply chain.

The banding together of industry leaders along with the guidance of intelligent organizations is essential to the success of sustainable fashion. Through this type of collaboration, brands can be held to certain standards and assisted in the process of meeting these standards. Additionally, many of the organizations aid consumers in supporting brands that do business responsibly. Both of these results are of great importance to the industry's success.

CHAPTER 9

INNOVATIONS WITHIN SUSTAINABILITY

This stop is one of my favorites of the entire trip. Here we get to explore all of the unique, resourceful, and truly genius ways people are changing not only the fashion industry, but the world.

In order for progress to occur within an industry, we need to constantly approach problems from new angles and work to discover creative ways to deal with the challenges we face. Today one of the greatest challenges the fashion industry faces is understanding how to continue to provide fashion to a growing population, remain profitable, and do so in a way that is sustainable for our future.

Innovation is the key in solving this issue and will be the catalyst for change in the fashion industry. One industry leader, Nike, eloquently states the issue with: "Nike believes the science is right, climate change is real, and we must take action now to power and protect the future of sport. This will require that the world radically redesign industrial systems and economies. It is not enough to adapt to what the future may bring, but that the future we want must be created through sustainable innovation."

Nike is finding a way to incite innovation among consumers with the Nike Circular Innovation Challenge. The innovation challenge is divided into two distinct parts that both feature cash prizes and partnership opportunities with the brand.

One part of the challenge is Design with Grind, which challenges consumers to think of creative new uses for Nike's recycled materials. Nike collects old footwear and combines them with manufacturing scraps to create a recycled material that in the past has been used to create over a billion square feet of sport surfaces including tracks, gym floors, and playgrounds.

The second challenge is called Material Recovery and encourages people to look for ways that the current model of recycled footwear can be improved. Innovations are expected to propose ideas that could replace current recycling practices, which would result in improvement of their supply chain.

Nike's approach to this challenge is an intelligent strategic move and good for the world. They have found a way to align the company's initiatives with the well-being of society. Additionally, the challenge serves as marketing tool to engage with consumers and build greater brand loyalty. This challenge is exemplary of something other brands should seek to do.

An often overlooked component of sustainable fashion that is rich with opportunity for innovation is in data analysis and reliable industry standards for sustainability performance. Because sustainability has so rapidly become a major concern for brands, the data needed to track and monitor the progress of the industry has lagged. One result of this has been the creation of the Sustainable Apparel Coalition.

The coalition is made up of a whole variety of brands ranging from Walmart to Burberry. This coalition represents the unifying of manufacturers, brands, and retailers to find reliable systems and metrics to measure sustainability. In gaining the ability to effectively measure sustainability, industry standards can be developed and brands can be held more accountable for their impact on the environment and society.

In response to this need for reliable measurement of brand

impact, the sustainable apparel coalition has developed the Higg Index. The Higg Index provides the fashion industry with the tools necessary to assess sustainability of their brand along every dimension of the supply chain from factories to retail storefronts. The Higg Index creates a common language within sustainability that will help allow consumers to make more informed purchasing decisions.

Another example of the push to create more reliable measurements for sustainability is the Environmental Profit and Loss (EP&L) Methodology. This methodology was developed by Kering, the parent company of brands such as Gucci and Alexander McQueen, and used first for its brand Puma. After successful use with Puma this methodology was then extended to all brands owned by the company.

An EP&L Methodology is essentially an analysis of a company that reveals the costs and benefits of the business' operations on the environment. This information can then be utilized by the brand to make decisions that are more sustainable. This type of measurement can also be useful in marketing and public relations for a company.

Being able to display to the public how your brand is making a difference is a valuable marketing tool as consumers move toward being more conscious of their buying decisions. Overall, improvements in a company's EP&L statistics can be a meaningful way to monetize their efforts and create more sustainable products.

An area where there has been a great deal of innovation is the textile field. Innovations within the textile field fall into two major categories. First is discovering new materials that are more sustainable for use in the creation of textiles. Second is the repurposing of old products into fashion pieces (the process of upcycling, which we discussed earlier).

The field of textiles is booming with innovative new ideas as brands around the world search for sustainable materials to use in their production. Hemp fiber is one example of a material beginning to see increased use. Hemp fiber is an antibacterial, durable, and naturally cooling material. On top of its excellent properties for clothing usage, it also requires very little water to grow and has no need for the use of herbicides, pesticides, or GMO seeds in production.

One of the only drawbacks to the material is its association with the production of marijuana. This negative association has caused many US brands to shy away from incorporating the material into their garments. However, this negative stigma is not relevant all over the world. Countries like China, where the industrial use of the cannabis plant has no legal restrictions, are producing hemp in great quantities for use in garments. It is possible that as marijuana becomes legalized in more and more states in the US we will see an increase in brands utilizing this dynamic material.

Another sustainable material being used and free of legal restrictions are stinging nettle fibers. These fibers are versatile as they are able to keep you warm in the winter and cool in the summer. Additionally, the production of this fiber needs far less pesticides and water than cotton requires. An interesting material beginning to be incorporated into textiles is coffee grounds. Companies like Singtex are using a mixture of coffee grounds and polymer to create yarn that has a variety of applications. The resulting textile has a natural anti-odor quality as well as a quick drying time.

Creative approaches to textile production extend into food as well. Fruits such as pineapples and bananas are being used today to make apparel. Through countless hours of research and experimentation, Ananas Anam has developed a suitable alternative to leather using pineapples. They take pineapple leaves, a natural by-product of the production of the fruit for the food industry, and break it down to create the base of their textile. The same process of utilizing waste from pineapple production is transferable to bananas. The stems of banana trees, which are normally just thrown away, can be used to create a durable material similar to bamboo. However, what makes the banana fibers even better is that they can be more easily molded into products as the material is naturally more flexible.

The innovations within textiles do not end with material creation but extend into how garments are dyed. The dye used in many fashion pieces today results in a great deal of chemical pollution and immense use of water. One sustainable fashion leader and biodesign expert, Natsai Audrey Chieza, is working on a system where bacteria-secreted pigments could be used to dye products.

Natsai is the director and founder of the biodesign lab Faber Futures, and her new method for dying garments could help solve the issue. Her dye requires less than seven ounces of water to dye a one-pound piece of silk. She puts this breakthrough in perspective in her citing of the following statistic: "A cotton T-shirt requires approximately 700 gallons of water to grow, produce and transport, with 20 percent or more of that water used in the dyeing process alone." Additionally, since her dye comes from bacteria, it is not toxic and would not contribute to the pollution of our waters.

The second category of innovation within textiles is repurposing old products into new ones. This process helps to reduce waste by minimizing the overwhelming volume of products that end up in landfills that could be used to make something new. Upcycling is different from recycling in that rather than reducing old products to lesser value, it adds value to the materials by repurposing them into products that can be sold at a greater value.

One company using this process in their business model is Looptworks. Looptworks' mission is embodied in their company slogan "excess made useful." An example of their business model at work is "Project Luv Seat." This project involved taking forty-three acres of leather from Southwest Airlines seats and making them into a bag collection where each bag was unique.

Rareform is another company that has embraced this model of upcycling. They take old billboards that would normally end up in landfills and turn them into a variety of products ranging from phone cases to duffel bags. Again, no two products they create are alike, which adds value for the customer who is getting their own unique version of the product.

Wolf and Lamb has taken a unique approach to this model as well. Founder Alison Reynolds travels to cities around the Midwest collecting old leather jackets and goods that have gone out of style. She then deconstructs these pieces and makes them into new products that are more aligned with the demands of modern fashion. Clearly, this model of upcycling is an important aspect in the sustainable fashion movement.

Another way to innovate is with new business models. I had the pleasure of having a conversation with a driven and intelligent woman named Kaveri Marathe regarding this topic. She started a company called Texiles, which seeks to reduce textile waste through a clothing pickup service.

The process is simple. All you do is sort through old clothes that you no longer have use for, schedule a pickup time (from your home), and Texiles will come and pick it up for you for a small fee. Texiles accepts just about any type of clothing so long as it has been washed. The clothes can be torn, tattered, stained, or just out of style.

The clothing the company collects can go to a variety of different uses including being resold, donated, or recycled. This business model is not only convenient for consumers but enables them to be environmentally conscious. Coming up with new business models like these is crucial to sustainability within the fashion industry.

Hopefully this helps give you an idea of the plethora of opportunity for innovation within the sustainable fashion space. This movement for innovation within the field can be continued with demand from consumers for more sustainable products and an understanding from apparel brands of the opportunities for growth that come with an investment in sustainable innovation.

CHAPTER 10

THE GLOBAL CHANGE AWARD

One commonly used and successful tactic to encourage innovation within an industry is to hold competitions with awards that will provide the opportunity for the winners to further pursue their innovative new idea. This model helps to motivate people within an industry to try and tackle some of the challenges the industry may be facing.

Providing the opportunity to join an accelerator program, receive expert coaching/consulting, and of course win grants to help fuel new venture makes entrepreneurs, creative thinkers, and companies more likely to pursue new technologies and ideas because there is additional assurance that their efforts will not be wasted. Global fashion leader H&M is putting this model into practice with their Global Change Award.

The H&M Foundation is a nonprofit global foundation funded by the owners of H&M in order to "drive long lasting positive change and improve living conditions by investing in people, communities and innovative ideas. Through partnerships with organizations around the globe, the H&M Foundation drives change within four focus areas—Education, Water, Equality and Planet."

The H&M Foundation initiated the innovation challenge in 2015 and collaborated with Accenture and KTH Royal Institute of Technology to bring the idea to life. This innovation challenge is the first of its kind in the fashion industry. The challenge looks for the best ideas that help the fashion industry move from a linear to circular industry.

A circular approach is one where valuable resources can be recovered and put into use again. A shift to this type of approach can be accomplished with disruptive new technologies and generating new models of business. The winning ideas help find ways to promote protecting the planet and ensuring fair working conditions for those in fashion supply chains. The H&M foundation takes no intellectual property rights because this initiative is not about their own profitability, but rather helping the whole industry move toward more sustainable production.

Each year the top five ideas are selected and then the public helps to decide how the grant will be split between the winners. The idea with the most votes receives just under $3.5 million, second place receives roughly $300,000 and then the third, fourth, and fifth place each receive almost $200,000.

Perhaps even more valuable than the cash prize, however, is the opportunity to participate in a year-long innovation accelerator program. This accelerator program helps the winners put their ideas into action by providing them with essential resources and expert guidance in the process.

The 2018 award winners were selected in March and feature some exciting breakthroughs for the fashion industry. The fifth place winner was Fungi Fashion with their MycoTEX. MycoTEX creates custom clothing from decomposable mushroom roots. The idea uses 3D technology to create the products without the need for cutting and sewing. One of the coolest features of this idea is the disposable nature of the products. When Fungi Fashion products are worn beyond use, they can simply be planted in the ground where they will decompose leaving behind no waste!

The fourth place winner features a similar model of waste-free materials. Smart Stitch's innovation is called Resortecs, which is a thread that simply dissolves at extremely high temperatures. This new thread is truly a breakthrough in the fashion industry because garments made from it can be used over and over. Rather than garments ending up in landfills, they can be melted down and made into a new piece repeatedly.

Two major concerns of current fashion production are the exorbitant water usage for common materials such as cotton and the water use and pollution associated with the dyeing process. Third place winner Algae Apparel tackles both of these issues with their Algalife. They have tapped into a previously unused material, algae, to create their garments. Algae is a renewable product that can be turned into both a fiber for apparel creation and an environmentally friendly dye.

In addition to the positive impacts on the environment, the use of algae also provides a major point of differentiation for brands utilizing it. When you wear the clothes made from algae, antioxidants, vitamins, and other nutrients are released from the clothes and enter your body through your skin. This means that not only do the pieces reduce environmental impact and look good, but they also make you feel good.

While it is important to find new materials to use in production, millions of garments in use today still do not feature these new technologies. The fashion industry needs a solution for all of these garments so they do not end up in landfills. Second place winning innovation, Swerea, has found a way to address this concern. They have discovered a way to use an environmentally friendly chemical to break down cotton and polyester blends into a fiber that can be used to make new products.

This cotton-polyester blend is one of the most common blends of materials used for clothing today and often requires the use of chemicals that are bad for the environment to be broken down. Now, with the help of Swerea, this issue is alleviated with an environmentally friendly process for breaking down this blend for future use.

The first place winner of this year's Global Change Award has found a way to make a positive impact both environmentally and socially. Crop-A-Porter has invented the Agraloop, which uses the waste created by crop production to produce a bio-fiber that can be turned into a textile fabric.

Normally the waste left behind from crop production is left to rot or burned, which releases carbon dioxide and methane gas into the air. The release of these gases contribute to climate change. The Agraloop has a positive environmental impact in terms of finding an environmentally friendly alternative material in addition to reducing the negative effects of another industry—the food industry.

The positive effects of this innovation do not stop with environmental impact but extend to social impact as well. Agraloop provides farmers with an additional revenue stream by finding a use for a material they previously would burn or leave to rot. Some examples of crops that Crop-A-Porter can use in their process are oil-seed flax, hemp, sugarcane, bananas, and pineapples.

The innovation challenge created by the H&M Foundation has already seen great success in propelling the fashion industry toward more sustainable production. Challenges like this one will help fuel progress in the industry and encourage creative thinking to solve some of the most pressing and challenging problems in the industry today.

CHAPTER 11

SUSTAINABLE FOOTWEAR

———

Over the course of our trip, footwear has mainly been combined with the fashion industry when we are discussing the negative impacts fashion can have. We have acknowledged some of the standout brands in apparel who are doing business in an ethical way—good for the environment and good for society.

But now it is time we make a stop to acknowledge some of the amazing footwear companies out there that are truly walking the talk.

One thing you'll notice is that these footwear lines span all different styles and functional purposes of the footwear market—demonstrating that ethical and sustainable business is not just some particular niche of the market. Ethical business can be achieved across the industry.

A leader in the sustainable fashion space, Everlane, helps affirm the idea that sustainability can be achieved across a variety of styles. They make a wide variety of footwear like boots, sandals, sneakers, and heels. They achieve sustainable business in a variety of ways—mainly revolving around the idea of radical transparency. They provide consumers with full transparency of their supply chains and the costs associated with them. Everlane only partners with ethical factories that are audited to ensure they are reducing environmental impact while paying fair wages to their workers.

The brand St. Agni is bringing the values of sustainability to a controversial topic in the sustainable fashion space—the leather industry. Leather is very controversial because the majority of leather goods makers produce their products using up a great deal of natural resources and creating a great deal of waste. Additionally, many people in the space promote vegan fashion and leather clearly does not fit this mold.

Some argue leather, if handled properly, can be very sustainable given its tremendously long product life cycle. St. Agni is doing their best to create leather goods in a sustainable way. They source their leather from a local farm so they can be sure of the humane treatment of the cows for consumption and leather. Additionally, their production is guided purely by demand to ensure they do not waste materials or goods. The final way they aim to reduce their impact is by using significantly less packaging that traditional footwear brands.

Another brand that has exploded onto the market in the past couple of years is Allbirds. The company was founded by native New Zealander, Tim Brown, who could not understand why Merino wool, something that any New Zealand native is very familiar with, was not being widely used in footwear and apparel production. The material is not only sustainable, but extremely comfortable. He teamed up with Joey Zwillinger, an engineer and renewables expert to make Allbirds a reality.

Besides using sustainable materials to create their products— the team at Allbirds has taken on additional endeavors in the pursuit of sustainability. For starters they are a B Corp certified company, which from our previous chapter about Organizations for Change, we know means that they redefine what it means to do business beyond a bottom line—prioritizing not just profits but the environment.

They also partner with a nonprofit, Soles4Souls, to help ensure the longest possible life cycle for their products as they aid in donating used shoes to communities in need. Finally, they flipped the idea of shoe packaging on its head. They created boxes from 90 percent post-consumer recycled cardboard that acts as a shoebox, shopping bag, or mailer—depending on your needs.

Action in the sustainability space many times comes from inspiring moments when people have the opportunity to see some of the damaging effects business can have when handled irresponsibly. The story for Veja, a French sneaker company founded in 2004, stays true to this. Founders Sébastien Kopp and François Morillon, cite their travels to orphanages and social projects in places like Mexico, Peru, Bolivia, and Brazil as their inspiration for their company. On these trips they saw the true side of globalization—the side many people do not know exists or do not want to acknowledge.

Today, Veja, is an example of a company embracing sustainability in every step of the supply chain. Their headquarters are fueled by energy from ENERCOOP (a cooperative of green electricity), they source their organic cotton from pesticide-, GMO-, and fertilizer-free farmers, and their products are assembled in Porto Alegre where their workers are paid above industry standards. They truly embrace what it means to be sustainable.

Like some other brands we have spoken about, they also do not keep stock of their products and produce based on demand. Additionally, they do not spend a single dollar on advertising. When asked, they respond that their focus is on providing consumers with an ethical and sustainable product for the cheapest possible price (oh, and that they think word of mouth is the best form of advertising). The founders also mention that they do not want to influence the debate about sustainability but are setting an example for what a company can do.

Another brand working passionately to create not only environmentally friendly shoes but to help fight the issue of plastic pollution is footwear and accessories company, The People's Movement. A series of events led Mark Wystrach to eventually cofound this company that is taking upcycled plastic bags from the ocean, pairing them with sustainable materials, and creating stylish eco-friendly shoes.

First was a heart attack right at the end of college—caused by an infection sustained from surfing in dirty water. Then Mark made a commitment to himself to live his life to the fullest, which led him to travel. During his travels he visited Bali, a beautiful country that is riddled with plastic.

Raised to respect the earth and leave it better than he found it—Mark knew he had to find a way to help combat the negative impact humans are having on the earth. Today he uses The People's Movement to achieve this goal. The People's Movement takes plastic removed from Bali and its shores to create its product. One particularly interesting organization that The People's Movement partners with is 5 Gyres.

The 5 Gyres is an organization that aims to enable action against the global health crisis of plastic pollution. Before diving a little deeper into the organization, I'll start by providing an explanation of the name. "A gyre is a large-scale system of wind-driven surface currents in the ocean. The gyres referred to in the name of our organization are the five main subtropical gyres—located in the North and South Pacific, the North and South Atlantic, and the Indian Ocean—which are massive, circular current systems."

You may be asking yourself about the relevance of these gyres. Well, within these gyres, plastic gets stuck. When I say stuck, I don't mean for a few hours or a few days. Plastic that ends up in the gyres takes over a decade to cycle back out—assuming it does not sink to the bottom or get eaten by marine life first.

The next logical question you are probably asking yourself is how much plastic has ended up in our oceans. The 2017 United Nations Clean Seas Campaign conducted research and came to the estimate that there are fifty-one trillion micro-plastic particles in our oceans today. For context that is five hundred times more than the number of stars in the galaxy. In terms of weight, it is estimated that there are roughly 270 metric tons' worth of plastic in our oceans.

Alright, I think you get the point. Plastic pollution is a major problem. Sorry for our brief detour away from sustainable fashion, but this is a super important issue not only in the sustainability space but to our entire society, and many fashion brands are playing a part in reducing the amount of plastic ending up in our environment.

One thing you may have noticed about the founding stories of the last two brands we just discussed is that they both were inspired by the travel of their founders. Travel changed their perspective because it allowed them to gain knowledge of what was going on in the world around them, but travel is not the only way we can gain this knowledge and change our perspectives. You are doing that right now! By reading this book you are able to gain knowledge of what is happening in an industry you undoubtedly play a role in—fashion. By gaining this knowledge you are empowering yourself to take action—whether that be in your everyday decisions or life path.

CHAPTER 12

CELEBRITY INFLUENCE

———

Have you ever purchased something purely because it was "cool"? How does a product or brand attain this distinction of being "hip" or "cool"? When a product or brand reaches this point, the primary consideration behind consumers' decisions to purchase it is no longer related to the quality of the product, but fueled by people's desire to fit in.

The most effective way for a brand to achieve this type of popularity is through celebrity endorsement. Take the case of Beats by Dre as an example. This company did not necessarily have a breakthrough in technology to help them dominate the headphones industry; rather, they gained endorsement from some of the biggest names in music such as Lady Gaga, Snoop Dogg, and Ludacris. But Beats did not stop there. They expanded into sports and had some of the most prominent figures in the athletics world showcasing their headphones including Lebron James and the vast majority of the US Olympians at the 2012 Olympics (who all received free customized pairs). All of this celebrity endorsement helped Beats to become synonymous with cool, leading them to control 60 percent of the 2.2-billion-dollar headphones industry.

So if this book is about sustainable fashion, why am I talking about Beats' domination of the headphone industry? The Beats success story proves that celebrity endorsement can be one of the most effective ways to not only reach consumers but also convert them to brand loyalists. And when someone is a brand loyalist, they can be prompted into action by their favorite brand. Celebrities today yield more power to influence people than ever before. Through the use of tools such as social media, celebrities can leverage their status and fame like never before. This is an important consideration as the sustainable fashion movement attempts to spread awareness and seeks continued growth.

The possibilities for spreading awareness of the movement when celebrities enter the equation are endless. What if Katy Perry sent out a tweet promoting slow fashion ideals? Well, it would reach her 108 million+ followers and millions more after those followers started retweeting to share with their friends. An Instagram post from Selena Gomez rocking apparel from a sustainable brand would be seen by her 130 million+ followers. The point is that celebrities have great influence over our culture, and this influence can be leveraged to promote movements, educate people, or support brands conducting business in ethical ways.

Because sustainable fashion is not just a product to push but an important social issue, many celebrities are already getting on board to help propel the movement. For example, Emma Watson is a well-known celebrity who has been a powerful voice for change in the fashion industry. She is a UN Women Goodwill Ambassador who advocates for women's rights and environmental consideration in the fashion industry. She is also the cofounder of her own site "FeelGood Style," which educates people on sustainable fashion and why it is important. Watson had this to say about her work with sustainable brands: "I will work for anyone for free if they're prepared to make their clothing fair trade and organic."

Pharrell Williams, an influential celebrity in both music and fashion, has joined the movement as well. Pharrell collaborated with G-Star RAW to release a line of jeans and denim products made from plastic pollution in oceans. Pharrell was able to strategically partner with the clothing brand because of his ownership stake in a startup called Bionic Yarn. This company helps cut down on plastic pollution by creating yarn from plastic waste. The yarn can be used in a wide variety of products from furniture and luggage to apparel.

One of the most prominent figures in the sustainable fashion space is Stella McCartney. McCartney owns her own brand of sustainable products, but also uses her power to enact change within other organizations. One such example was her partnership with H&M that resulted in a collaborative line. In reference to the collaboration, she said, "We insisted on things. We insisted on guidelines. We insisted that it was organic and sustainable. I don't think that had happened to them before so that was brought to their attention, and the success of it—the desirability was a nice eye opener for them, to be able to see that it sold out in four seconds."

Emma Watson, Pharrell Williams, and Stella McCartney all provide examples of how partnerships with celebrities can be utilized to promote sustainability in the fashion world. Their celebrity status can help to not only promote brands, but further encourage people to become informed and more conscious of the issue.

CHAPTER 13

LEVERAGING PSYCHOLOGY IN SUSTAINABILITY

———

One thing I have been wondering is why many people in the United States today do not view climate change as a major issue. As a result of millions and millions of people either not believing in or not viewing climate change as important, there is less consumer demand for companies that embrace sustainability. Without demand from consumers, companies are not motivated to pursue these practices. So why is it that some people do not share the same concern for the fate of our planet? It's something that affects all of us, so it seems counterintuitive to not be concerned about it. Doesn't it? These questions have nagged at me, and so I decided to look into the psychology of sustainability.

In my searching I found a woman named Simran Sethi who had these same questions and was able to chip away at why many people disregard climate change. Simran is a journalist and educator who focuses on food, sustainability, and social change. She gave a TED Talk that helped me understand the psychology behind sustainability a little more.

At first Simran thought the answer to getting people to care about sustainability was to provide them with the facts. If people knew some of the facts about human-induced climate change, they would care about the issue. However, she learned that bombarding people with information was not the answer. In her TED Talk she said, "Psychologists have almost no evidence that information changes people's decision-making. We tend to believe the facts and embrace the facts that already confirm our world view. It's called confirmation bias. We tend to disregard the facts that do not align with our view. This is how we make sense of the world."

So then she turned to trying to focus on the business side of things. She would make the business case for why certain sustainability practices make sense for companies to adopt because of their ability to improve efficiencies and increase their bottom line. While this can be somewhat effective, it still does not get through to everyone. So how can you get through to people?

The key, she discovered, is to provide context to the threat of climate change by making it something people can relate to and understand in the framework of their own lives. In her talk she mentions how we as a human species did not evolve to deal with problems as complex as climate change. We cannot fully comprehend issues of this magnitude or all of the consequences of it. She cites the findings of Harvard researcher Daniel Gilbert to help illustrate the point further. As humans we have a finite number of things we can worry about. We only respond to threats that are instant, imminent, personalized, or in some way repulsive to us. All threats that fall outside of this category do not register the same need for action.

So what does this mean relative to sustainable fashion? This idea of putting things in a context that people can relate to on a personal level can be useful for anyone trying to help propel the idea of sustainability in fashion. It can be useful as brands try to educate and engage their consumers to shift mindsets or change behaviors. It can be helpful for sustainability teams within companies to consider as they try to influence different departments within an organization to embrace more responsible practices. It can be helpful for companies in aligning their mission with the values of their employees. Overall, I think this exploration of our human psychology is a key consideration for the sustainable fashion movement. This ability to take a large-scale problem and boil it down to something people can relate to is a difficult but necessary endeavor.

On my journey, I came across some research completed by the Minnesota Pollution Center that provides some insights about psychology specific to sustainability. The findings in this report can be used as a tool for empowering brands who want to act sustainability. The first insight is working to make sustainable behavior the social default.

A good example the report gives to illustrate this idea is in household energy usage. When consumers were asked what factors would be most likely to affect their energy usage they rated "how much their neighbors were cutting back" as the least likely to affect them below environmental impact, money savings, and how-to instructions. However, the results showed that this was actually the only thing that resulted in people reducing their electricity usage.

Human beings are social creatures and are naturally influenced by what other people are doing, whether we realize it or not. Therefore, we need to work toward establishing sustainable behavior as a social norm. We have already seen this taking place in the fashion industry when some brands champion their sustainability practices. As more and more companies adopt more sustainable approaches, it forces the competition to do the same in order to stay relevant in the marketplace.

Another insight from the report was the same idea Simran was promoting—emphasizing the importance of personal relevance. This report details how one way to make things more personally relevant to people is to not frame things in the context of it being good or bad for the environment. When sustainability is positioned as something for the environment, it creates a false division between people and nature.

The environment and humans are intertwined and have direct effects on one other. As we pollute and damage the earth, we feel the consequences of these actions. Another way to keep things personally relevant is by focusing on local issues and the ways that sustainable action can impact people's everyday lives.

The report talks about the idea of "making hidden information visible," meaning it is important to find ways to make the effects of climate change perceivable to people. The inability of various environmental hazards such as air pollution and soil erosion to be detected with our own senses and the need for science to uncover these issues make them seem less real. This can be overcome with things like graphic displays, concrete images, and real-world demonstrations. Finding creative ways to exemplify abstract concepts will help make people more willing to embrace sustainable practices.

These serve as a few examples of the ways we can use our current understandings of human psychology as a meaningful way to promote sustainability. By taking into account our natural human biases and tendencies, we can better create an environment where sustainable practices are embraced.

CHAPTER 14

WHAT IS THE SLOW FASHION MOVEMENT?

———

The way the majority of the fashion industry functions today revolves around a model commonly referred to as fast fashion. The fast fashion model is a system where retailers rush to recreate the latest trends seen on the runways at the cheapest possible cost so they can mass produce them and sell them to eager consumers looking to keep up with the newest trends for the season.

The model encourages people to consume far more apparel than they need. The idea is that you can buy the latest trend for cheap, wear it a few times, throw it out at the end of the season (because not only is it out of style, but also likely falling apart), and then this cycle is repeated the following season.

So what's the problem? Why does it matter if people want to be continually updating their wardrobe? The repercussions of this type of buying behavior are immense in magnitude. The fast fashion model negatively impacts both the environment and the workers in factories that are producing the clothes. We already know some of the negative ways fashion can affect our environment including pollution of our water with chemicals used in dyes, the gobbling up of precious natural resources, and the wasting of billions of gallons of water each year.

Now imagine how much this effect is worsened when a portion of the industry is doing this to create new lines of clothing not just for every season but for every few weeks within each season. In terms of impact on workers, the demand to create these pieces at the lowest possible cost continues to drive wages of factory workers down to levels that are not suitable for them to provide for themselves or their families.

Despite the daunting nature of this task, some people fight back against the harmful fast fashion model. The term slow fashion movement was first coined by Kate Fletcher, a professor at the Sustainable Fashion Centre. This is a movement of consumers, designers, retailers, and manufacturers who are all making the commitment to a more sustainable fashion industry.

A major component of the movement is shifting the mind-set that consumers have when approaching their fashion purchases. Leaders in the sustainable fashion space have been encouraging investing in essential wardrobe pieces that are of high quality and can be used for a prolonged period of time. Rather than spending money on cheap clothes each season, instead spend that money on clothing that can last for years. Consumers making this shift to minimize their clothing consumption and invest in the clothes they do purchase will help the slow fashion movement grow.

The slow fashion movement is not meant to just be the opposite of fast fashion. This movement is about the industry making more conscientious decisions along all dimensions of the supply chain. A study featured in the *Journal of Retailing and Consumer Services* detailed the slow fashion process as products move from retailer to consumer. In the design stage, brands can focus on sustainability and consider the most strategic way to go about creating their products and minimizing impact. The following stage, when production has begun, is where quality and craftsmanship are key. Creating durable products that will last customers longer periods of time is a key component of the movement. The final stage in the process is consumption, where educating consumers is the priority. As discussed, consumers need a shift in mindset to invest in their clothing in order for this model to succeed.

For the movement to fully develop and become a suitable alternative to fast fashion, researchers from the Master's

Programme in Strategic Leadership towards Sustainability in Sweden have identified "sustainable values" that can be used to guide supply chain decisions. The first value is seeing the bigger picture.

Brands need to recognize how interconnected we all are and that the decisions made by industry leaders will influence the decisions other brands make. One brand's actions can have a serious effect on our environment, but the sum of all brands' supply chain decisions can cause irreversible damage if these decisions are made without seriously contemplating their impact on our long-term future.

Another value is slowing down consumption. We need to slow down consumption of our finite resources to a level where the earth can keep pace with our consumption. Less use of natural resources will allow the earth to replenish itself and provide us with the resources we need.

Additionally, the researchers listed respect for people as a must-have value for the slow fashion movement. Respecting people within the fashion industry means ensuring that all workers have safe working conditions and are paid fair wages.

Some companies are even taking additional steps to support local communities like Toms Shoes, which provides skill development to local communities.

The researchers do not forget to mention profitability as one of the key values for the movement. It is important for brands to focus on sustaining profitability because it allows them to grow and expand their socially conscious ways of doing business.

The slow fashion movement is a sustainable alternative to the way the industry currently operates and is garnering more and more popularity. As consumers' mindsets shift and brands adopt new ways of doing business, we will continue to see improvements of the fashion industries impact on both society and the environment.

CHAPTER 15

THE GROWTH OF APPAREL RENTAL

———

One trend that is disrupting the fashion industry is the rapid growth of apparel rental. The apparel rental model allows consumers to rent specific pieces for a set fee or pay a monthly subscription for access to a selection of garments each month. Companies such as Rent the Runway have popularized this business model of offering consumers the option to rent clothing ranging from high end luxury brands to collections of everyday wear pieces. This rental model helps to greatly reduce waste and embraces the sharing economy we have seen growing in recent years.

Millennials are greatly responsible for the growth of this trend as it aligns with their mindset and lifestyle choices. A study conducted by Coresight Research identified factors that help explain the popularity of this trend among millennials. The three main factors they discovered were the Instagram effect, an increased focus on experience, and budget consciousness.

The Instagram effect has been created by the growth of celebrity culture and selfies. Millennials have a great desire to be viewed as living fun and exciting lives. Wearing a wide variety of name brands is part of this desired persona. Renting clothing makes attaining this persona much more feasible for young people who often do not have as much discretionary income to spend on their wardrobe.

Additionally, millennial consumers on average place a greater value on experience as opposed to material possessions. Saving money on their wardrobe allows them to invest more in other things, such as experiences. In a study done by Eventbrite and Harris Poll, they found that 78 percent of millennials would rather spend their money on some sort of experience than buying a product.

Finally, being budget conscious is a contributing factor because millennials do not see the value in making large investments in higher end clothing that will only be worn for a few occasions.

Other factors discussed in the study that affect the growth of rentals among this demographic are decluttering, the popularity of fast fashion, and environmental sustainability. Millennials have a desire to declutter their closest and monetize the clothing that sits in their closets unused so they can spend this money elsewhere. The rental model allows consumers to engage in the fast fashion trend of varying their styles greatly without significant investments in their wardrobe and the negative impacts on the environment.

Sustainability is the final factor that draws millennial interest in this business model. In a study conducted by Nielsen in 2015, 75 percent of millennials are willing to pay more for a product that was produced in a sustainable way.

These factors as well as the three discussed in the paragraph above can help to shed light on why rental popularity among millennials is the largest contributor to the growth of the apparel rental industry.

The growth of this industry can additionally be contributed to a shift in consumer mindset. Consumers were already beginning to shift their purchasing behavior, and the apparel rental industry has not only capitalized on this change but contributed to the continuation of this changing mindset. Emmanuelle Brizay, cofounder of apparel rental site Panoply City said, "Renting changes the consumer's relationship with clothes. One continues to buy them but you also can have more fun. Instead of buying an umpteenth black coat for the winter, with the same money you can change the color every week."

The rise of the sharing economy has caused consumers to place far less emphasis on ownership and open their minds to the idea of renting products. Marshal Cohen, the chief industry analyst at the NDP group—a company that conducts industry analysis to uncover market trends—commented on the shift in the apparel industry. "Rental has gone from a dirty, used, and low-end perspective to an even cleaner, easier, more convenient way to shop luxury."

This consumer shift away from ownership is not unique to the fashion industry. One such example is a streaming service like Spotify, which disrupted the music industry by allowing consumers to pay a subscription fee to get access to their music instead of buying songs on an individual basis.

Clearly, numerous factors can be attributed to the growing success of the rental model in the fashion industry. This shift is an important facet of the sustainable movement because it is a useful tool in the battle to slow down fast fashion. Millennial consumers are playing a large role in the success of this model. Additionally, the shift in consumer mindset is both helping the success of this new business model and continuing to influence consumers' buying behavior.

STOP #4

CHANGE IS POSSIBLE

So what have we covered?

Well, first we took a look at the fashion industry as a whole. Our next stop explored a little further into why the fashion industry needs to see change with some touching stories. From there we moved into some of the ways this change is happening and how it can continue to occur. What's next, you ask?

Our next and final stop shows that change within the industry is possible. We will explore topics like brands transitioning to sustainability, brands that are exemplary of sustainability, what steps along the value chain brands can take, and how an event we discussed prior influenced the industry.

This stop in our journey is meant to show that yes—the fashion industry can change… and is changing.

CHAPTER 16

TRANSITIONING TO A SUSTAINABLE BRAND

———

Sustainability for a company in the fashion industry is not yet a standard. It is also definitely not something that will just come about naturally. In order for a company in the fashion industry to engage in responsible behavior that takes into account the impact their practices have on both the environment and its workers, it must make a full commitment to sustainable practices.

Sustainability is not something that just comes easily. As I learned in my conversations with sustainability representatives at companies like Patagonia and Levi Strauss & Co, sustainability requires an ongoing commitment. So much development and innovation are occurring, and companies must remain committed to ensuring they stay up to date with the newest and most cutting-edge practices if they really want to reduce their negative impact the most.

Sustainability is usually thought to be an unprofitable endeavor. However, this is simply not the case. Sustainability can be incorporated into a business strategy or supply chain operation in a variety of ways to net the company profits. The pursuit of profits and sustainable practices does not have to be mutually exclusive. Some businesses utilize sustainability efforts to improve their overall efficiencies and cut costs in the long run. Others may use it as a point of differentiation in brand positioning and marketing efforts to capitalize on the growth of socially minded consumers.

One of the most important points I have found in my research is that just because a company is not sustainable in the present moment does not mean they cannot begin to make changes within their supply chain and practices in order to become more sustainable. Because sustainability involves almost every dimension of a business' functions, this change takes time and a full commitment from the company. However, the large scope means there are a variety of potential starting points.

Companies can slowly adapt their practices based on what makes the most sense for their unique situation. A quote I find very relevant to this idea is one from internet entrepreneur and author Jason Calacanis. "You have to have a big vision and take very small steps to get there. You have to be humble as you execute but visionary and gigantic in terms of your aspiration. In the internet industry, it's not about grand innovation. It's about a lot of little innovations: every day, every week, every month, making something a little bit better."

Although he may be speaking about a different industry, the same ideas apply to brands trying to embrace sustainability in fashion. Brands need to embrace this idea of constantly trying to innovate and take steps in the right direction every day.

To begin the conversation of shifting to sustainability, I will speak about my findings with a company that is well-known across the globe, Nike. Nike struggled in the past with some difficult hits to its reputation because of the media exposure of labor abuses and environmental impact in the 1990s. Articles written by *Time* and videos aired on major media outlets such as ESPN and CBS inflicted some damaging blows to the company's image.

Additionally, a troubling report constructed by Ernst & Young was discovered featuring statistics such as "77 percent of workers at a supplier factory had respiratory problems and were being exposed to carcinogens 177 times above the legal level." After evading the issue for a little, Nike knew it had to make a change and face some of the troubling things occurring in the company.

To tackle the issue, they called upon Hannah Jones, who joined the company as director of government and community affairs and is now the chief sustainability officer and VP of the Innovation Accelerator. Hannah commented on the shift the company made, saying, "We really started to look into what things within our business we could change or do better, such as our purchasing practices and teaching designers how to design with sustainability in mind." Following this analysis, sustainability "moved from being a risk and reputation function to being a business lever function to being an innovation function."

The company shifted its strategy in three major ways. The first was a commitment to transparency of its practices. The second was building partnerships with other companies in the industry that were also making commitments to things like better rights for their workers. One such example is their cofounding of the Fair Labor Association. The Fair Labor Association works to improve working conditions across the industry by advocating on workers' behalf and providing training on management and best practices to brands.

The final shift in strategy was tying sustainability with innovation. The company began to utilize innovation as a means for them to find more sustainable practices. This not only helps Nike but sets an example for others in the industry that sustainability can be good for a company and serve as a tool for successful business.

Nike serves as an example that a large global brand can make the shift to sustainability. When Hannah Jones was asked what she is most proud of from her time at Nike, she said the following, "I never know how to answer this question; you have milestones, but what matters more is the journey. How is this becoming the core value of how we think about our roles at Nike collectively? It's hard to measure any individual milestones or thrust a barometer into the organization and tell you exactly where we're at. I can tell you though that with the work I see coming out now, I've never been prouder to work at Nike than I am today."

Another brand that serves as an example of how companies can make this shift is the Mara Hoffman brand. She was inspired after the birth of her child to consider the impact the fashion industry is having on the environment. She is quoted in *Vogue* magazine as saying, "Here I am as a manufacturer and I'm making things [every season], but my son and his generation are the ones who will have to deal with all this stuff. We've been making things too rapidly, and there's too much of it."

Mara Hoffman also discussed how the shift to becoming a

sustainable brand is not something that just happens overnight. With so many different suppliers and dimensions of a fashion supply chain, the process of becoming sustainable is ongoing. One of the first changes Hoffman made was in her swimwear collection. In her swimwear she started using recycled Nylon and digital prints to help reduce waste.

She also realizes that this shift in her company's mission is going to require a shift in the messaging she uses with consumers. In order to embrace sustainability, Mara is focusing on the quality of her products and encouraging consumers to invest with her. She explains: "I want to push this idea of spending a little bit more with me, and you can re-wear [the clothes] so you don't have to buy so much. Uniform dressing is cool—that's what we have to start telling people." While this shift in consumer mindset away from the fast fashion model will be difficult, it is an important aspect of the sustainability movement in the apparel industry.

A final story of a brand making the shift sustainability is Evan Toporek's brand Alternative Apparel. In my conversation with Evan, we talked about how the sub brand of the company Alternative Earth began to become the essence of the entire company. Alternative Apparel started to embrace sustainable practices in every aspect of their business. Some environmentally friendly practices that Alternative Apparel now utilizes include using a tri-blend for their garments that consists of organic cotton and recycled polyester from recycled plastic and using low-impact dye on their fabrics to reduce pollution of toxic dyes.

Evan also spoke about the importance of the social dimension of his business. Alternative Apparel ensures that all their factories are WRAP certified. WRAP stands for Worldwide Responsible Accredited Production and was a response from the fashion industry to issues occurring in factories abroad like child labor and unsafe working conditions.

Evan said when you are a sustainable brand, you do not get transaction by transaction credit for it. Rather you are rewarded by the loyalty of socially minded consumers who want to buy products from a brand whose values align with their own.

There are some key takeaways from looking at these three brands. First you can see that the shift to sustainability can happen regardless of the size of the company. Nike, Mara Hoffman, and Alternative Apparel all represent vastly different sized companies, but all three have been able to make this shift.

Second, making a commitment to sustainability is not a shift that can immediately happen. The process of making sure your business is minimizing its impact on the environment and also treating its workers fairly is a gradual process that takes time, monitoring, and consistent effort.

Finally, these companies show that sustainability can indeed be a profitable initiative for a company to embrace. It can result in increased efficiencies within a supply chain and a point of differentiation in the marketplace.

CHAPTER 17

PULSE REPORT: ACTIONABLE CHANGES ALONG THE VALUE CHAIN

———

Hey, look! It's the Pulse Report again! Remember earlier in our journey when I was raving on about how great this report was? Well, here it is again.

As a refresher, when we looked at the report before, we learned about the various steps along the value chain from design and development to the end of use for a product. Now for this chapter we will use the Pulse Report to identify the actionable steps companies can take at each stage in this value chain to transition to more sustainable practices.

The report provides minimum requirements at each step for the low performers to improve practices and close the gap between them and top performers. Additionally, the report describes current best practices in the industry, which can serve as long-term goals for many brands. In this chapter, I will address the minimum requirements for brands because this change is the most imperative in the industry today.

In the design and development phase, the product design teams can do a great deal to contribute to sustainability because the decisions they make in this crucial first step can positively influence various other stages of the product creation and life cycle. Brands can improve sustainability when designers consider optimization of the materials they use. Companies can enable their design and development teams by providing them with the information they need to make responsible decisions about the fibers and mixes they use in for products.

By providing the right data and coupling this with recommendations of possible alternative materials, designers will be able to make better educated decisions. If brands are in need of more guidance to achieve sustainable practices at this stage, they can turn to TED (Textiles Environment Design), an organization that researches the best practices for incorporating sustainability in design. Their research can be a useful tool for designers in this often complex stage.

Another actionable change during this step is engaging in a durability testing process to make sure products are created for long-term use. Finally, brands can limit their sample creation and allocation in this step through proper research and planning.

Brands can improve the raw materials stage's environmental impact by requiring certain certifications of their suppliers to ensure they are using sustainable materials. In addition to this step, they can put systems in place to track the impact of their materials use.

In terms of labor issues, requiring suppliers to get certifications in order to ensure they meet certain standards is again effective. Various organizations monitor suppliers and certify those that are providing their workers with safe conditions and living wages while ensuring the absence of child labor.

One company that is helping to make advances in the raw materials stage is Worn Again. This startup identified a major problem in the marketplace when it comes to the fashion industry. We are throwing away almost as much as we are creating. On their site, they detail the problem by explaining that we make fifty-five million tons of polyester and cotton each year but discard fifty million tons of textiles each year.

So what if we used the abundance of materials that end up in landfills to manufacture new garments rather than constantly creating more? Worn Again addressed this with their new textile-to-textile recycling technology. Their technology breaks down old polyester and cotton garments and creates new materials that can reenter the supply chain. Startups like this one are finding unique ways to reduce waste that can help fashion brands improve their sustainability at this initial stage of product creation.

For the processing stage, brands can work to reduce their environmental footprint by fully enforcing a policy of not using restricted substances. Many of the chemicals that are commonly used at this stage fall into this category. Nike embraced this type of action in their 2016 Super Bowl collection when they partnered with the Dutch company DyeCoo.

DyeCoo used a new type of dyeing process that utilized pressurized CO_2 so that zero water was necessary in the dyeing process. Another action brands can take is providing targets and guidelines regarding their chemical usage.

Finally, fashion companies should conduct research to find the most reliable and responsible suppliers for this stage. After these supplies have been identified, they can build long-term relationships with them to aid in future collaboration. In terms of social issues, brands can track and monitor their labor conditions to make sure their employees are not being exposed to hazardous materials or poor/dangerous working conditions.

One clear path that brands can take during manufacturing to improve this stage is increasing transparency. Brands can accomplish this by sending representatives to their factories to assess the factories' performance on sustainability in terms of both environmental impact and labor conditions. The brand could use its own sustainability experts to conduct this auditing process or a third-party option.

Another way brands can improve at this stage is reducing packaging waste. This option is useful because while materials being used in garment production cannot be changed at this stage, it is easily possible to use new processes of packaging and better materials for packaging.

The next step in the process is the transportation of the products. While this is the fashion industry's highest scoring stage in terms of Pulse Score (just as a reminder, a higher score is better), there is still room for improvement. To improve at this stage, brands should take steps to measure and track the impact per garment in order to monitor how efficiently they are transporting their goods.

This would also give them a benchmark to work from as they try to increase their efficiency. Companies should collaborate with the teams that transport the goods to find ways to maximize their transport space. Maximizing transport space will then lead to less vehicles being used in the process.

At the retail stage, brands can try to communicate to consumers what they can do to reduce their environmental footprint. Consumers have the ability to make a very large impact in reducing the waste creation, water consumption, energy usage, etc. that results from the fashion industry just by slightly adjusting their behavior.

Since retail storefronts are a brand's main point of contact with customers, they should try to leverage this stage. If more companies take on initiatives to educate their customers, it could become more of an industry standard. Additionally, companies can reduce energy usage and water consumption within their storefronts.

Once the product has been passed on to the consumer, brands can still make a difference in many ways. At the consumer use stage, brands can contribute to sustainability by providing their customers with materials to extend the life of products such as replacement yarns and buttons. Brands can go beyond these simple measures and provide additional repair services when garments tear.

One brand that is really excelling in this stage is Patagonia with their Worn Wear program. This program has multiple facets that contribute to the long-term use of their products. One thing they offer consumers is the option to buy gently used clothing for discounted prices. Additionally, they offer to buy back products from consumers and give them credit for these garments that can be used on new Patagonia gear.

If you do not want to part with your piece, you can also get it repaired for free. Patagonia's program involves forty-five full-time repair technicians who perform over forty thousand repairs a year. On the Worn Wear site, they also have product care guides and forums to help consumers learn how to prolong the life of their products through proper care and simple at-home repair options.

One of the coolest parts of the program is the stories section of the Worn Wear site. Here they feature testimonials from customers about the life of their products and what their special Patagonia pieces mean to them. This part of the site is great because it allows Patagonia to engage with their consumer base and promotes the company's values of not creating waste by getting the most out of their products.

Another way companies can educate consumers at this stage of the process is with the tags they place in garments. By providing information on tags about how consumers can care for and wash their products with the lowest environmental impact, brands can continue to reduce their industry's environmental impact.

Once consumers have finished with their garment, it moves to the end of use stage. Brands can still help them to act more responsibly by providing recycling options for their clothes and footwear at this time. By putting the infrastructure in place for consumers to recycle their clothes, brands are enabling their consumers to be more environmentally responsible. Additionally, they are potentially gaining materials useful for future production. By doing something as simple as putting donation bins in stores, brands promote recycling and provide their customers with an easy solution for their old clothes.

The purpose of this chapter was to demonstrate the very feasible steps that can and should be taken by brands in the fashion industry to reduce the entire industry's impact. This is by no means a comprehensive list for what brands should be doing, but these actions would be good initial steps for companies in the space to take. I have also detailed the work of a few companies to show some of the progress fashion brands are making and to provide examples of startups and organizations that can act as resources to fashion brands.

CHAPTER 18

BANGLADESH FACTORY COLLAPSE IMPACT

———

Earlier in the book, I touched on the tragic incident of a factory that collapsed in Bangladesh. While this incident was both horrifying and unacceptable, there was a silver lining to the situation in regards to the wake-up call it gave the fashion industry. The constant disregard of worker safety coupled with the tragedy of the event caused the fashion industry to take action to prevent something like this from happening again.

In this chapter we will first look at some of the progress that has been made in Bangladesh when it comes to garment production. Afterward, we will address areas where there is still room for improvement.

The building collapse of the factory in Bangladesh resulted in the creation of two different agreements—the Alliance for Bangladesh Worker Safety and the Accord on Fire and Building Safety in Bangladesh. The Alliance for Bangladesh Worker Safety was a five-year commitment that was signed in 2013. It was intended to improve worker safety in the ready-made garment industry by doing the following: "upgrading factories, educating workers and management, empowering workers, and building institutions that can enforce and maintain safe working conditions throughout Bangladesh." The means through which they plan to accomplish these aforementioned goals involves five strategic pillars including remediation, standards and inspections, training, sustainability, and worker empowerment.

The purpose of the Accord on Fire and Building Safety in Bangladesh is to provide workers with an environment where they can feel safe and not have to fear the possibility of fires in the factory or entire buildings collapsing. It involves more than two hundred apparel companies from over twenty different countries.

Six key components to the agreement are stated on their website. First, the agreement was five years long, legally binding, and between the two major players—brands and trade unions. The second component states there must be an independent inspection program paid for by brands. To ensure there is no collusion and the inspection program truly is independent, it must involve both workers and trade unions.

The third component focuses on disclosure as brands are required to submit factory inspection reports and any corrective action plans that may be applicable. The fourth part is about ensuring there are sufficient funds (signing brands held accountable) available for maintaining sourcing relationships.

The fifth component is perhaps one of the most impactful. It ensures there is a democratically elected health and safety committee in every single factory to make sure that health and safety risks are acted on. Finally, the accord includes an extensive training program that is devoted to worker empowerment. Through worker empowerment programs like this, workers can speak up about their complaints and exercise their right to not work in unsafe conditions.

According to reports, the accord has seen some success in increasing the safety of workers, and roughly 2.5 million workers are now working in safer conditions as a result of it. In terms of building conditions, 97,000 of 123,000 hazards in Bangladeshi factories have been handled and approved. Another 12,000 have been handled, but await approval.

Other areas where improvement can be seen include using buildings intended for garment production and the creation of some unions. The number of garment factories in multi-purpose factories has dropped 51 percent from 155 to 79. This is good because the trend of putting garment factories in buildings that were intended to be something like an office space was a root cause of the danger many workers were being put in.

All of these efforts have definitely made a difference in the lives of Bangladeshi garment workers. Since the disaster in April 2013 roughly forty Bangladeshi garment workers have died (mostly in fires), which is a significant improvement from the nearly five hundred Bangladeshi workers who were killed in fires and disasters from 2006-2010.

While all of this progress is great and seeing brands and the industry as whole moving in this direction is exactly what we want, some definite room for improvement remains in the industry. Initially after the incident, the Bangladeshi ready-made garment industry was put under a microscope and every component of its operations were subject to scrutiny. This caused immediate improvements in the wages of workers in 2013.

However, since this initial spike, wages have not continued to improve to keep pace with the rate of inflation. When Bangladesh is compared to a major competitor in the garment industry labor force, Vietnam, you see that Vietnamese workers are paid on average more than double what Bangladeshi workers are paid. Another trend we have seen moving in the wrong direction is the pressures put on factories to speed up production processes at all costs. The amount of time a worker is given to complete a production process has fallen by 8.1 percent from 2011 to 2015, putting more pressure on the workers. With this increased pressure, we have seen an increased need for workers to work overtime to meet this demand. Sadly, many workers do not receive proper pay for these overtime hours.

There is a great demand from consumers for overall better transparency throughout the industry. However, this push for greater transparency has been met with some resistance. A coalition of labor and human rights groups and global unions has contacted seventy-two major apparel and footwear companies, and only seventeen of them have agreed to implement the transparency pledge.

In detailing some of the specific companies cooperating, an NPR article stated: "Companies such as Nike, Patagonia and H&M Group are among the seventeen committing to adhere to the transparency pledge by the end of 2017. Others, such as Columbia Sportswear and the Walt Disney Co., which publish names and addresses of supplier factories, are acknowledged in the report as 'moving in the right direction.' Companies listed in the 'No Commitment to Publish

Supplier Factory Information' category include Hugo Boss, Mango and Walmart."

Some companies fear signing the transparency pledge because they believe it will put them at a competitive disadvantage and is anti-competition. Others, like Walmart, cite their own transparency pledges that they have in place as enough and therefore refuse to involve themselves in others.

Transparency, especially for these massive global players, is key to keeping them honest. When the factory building collapsed, many fashion brands denied any connection to the situation even though they were using the building as a supplier. Many of the brand's representatives were not lying but simply uninformed. The fact was that many of the brand's supply chains had become so large and out of control they had trouble keeping track of each stage of their supply chain.

In conclusion we can see that while tragic, the Bangladesh Factory Collapse in 2013 did a great deal as a catalyst for progress in the industry. Clear room for improvement still exists and people's outrage from the April 2013 tragedy will continue to fuel the push toward safer conditions for workers not just in Bangladesh, but all over the world.

CHAPTER 19

HOW A GLOBAL BRAND INCORPORATES SUSTAINABILITY

How can you tell if someone is passionate about something? Plenty of people will tell you are they are passionate about a sport, job, cause, hobby, etc. but in my own personal experiences someone telling you they are passionate about something does not necessarily mean they are. For me, determining if someone is passionate about something has nothing to do with the words they say, but rather the way in which they talk about their passion.

Have you ever spoken with someone and been inspired by their commitment and passion? Well I can say with confidence that after my conversation with Kelsey Pecherer, manager of sustainable business and marketing at Levi Strauss & Co., I have had this experience. Through our conversation, it was abundantly clear to me the commitment she has to sustainable business and the passion she has for the work she does. This chapter helps show how passionate individuals working within the framework of larger organizations can enact change. Many of the individuals we have discussed so far have enacted change through companies they founded themselves, but this chapter is different.

Kelsey has worked in the sustainability space her entire career and is very well educated on the topic. Before coming to Levi Strauss, she worked in the environmental compliance space. An example of this work includes helping a farm take the necessary steps to gain certification as an organic farm. After this stint in the compliance space, she returned to business school to get her MBA so she could more effectively help businesses incorporate sustainability into their operations.

In her time working with businesses, she came to a frustrating realization. She explains, "The common theme I was finding was that sustainability for so many companies is something that just gets put on the back burner. It's not a priority to incorporate it into the business model." This realization was one of the driving factors in accepting her position at Levi Strauss. In her research and interactions with the Levi Strauss team, she found that for them sustainability was not an afterthought.

Kelsey explained to me how at Levi Strauss sustainability is a primary commitment. The value system they have in place within the company naturally allows for sustainability to become embedded within its business model. Additionally, Levi Strauss, unlike many other companies who use sustainability as one of the points of differentiation, does not engage in the act of "greenwashing."

Greenwashing is when companies use advertising and marketing to deceive consumers and make them think they are more environmentally friendly than they really are. Proof that Levi Strauss does not engage in Greenwashing can be exemplified in Kelsey's collaboration with the marketing department (something we will get to later in this chapter).

Since greenwashing is a term we have not discussed before, I want to explain why this practice can be so harmful. First and foremost, it is deceitful and preys on socially conscious consumers. It also allows companies that are not making investments in sustainability to make similar claims as ones that actually are. This discourages brands from making the necessary investments in sustainability and detracts from one of their points of differentiation within the marketplace.

At Levi Strauss Kelsey has a dynamic and unique position

as a manager of sustainable business. She looks for ways the company can embed more sustainable practices within every aspect of their business operations. Levi Strauss has a team of sustainability experts ranging from water consumption and energy emissions to labor issues. They all research and discover the newest technologies and innovations occurring in the space. Kelsey takes these practices and works with people on the product team and within the supply chain to see how these practices can be fused into their operations.

One of the Kelsey's biggest focuses is helping Levi Strauss move to a more circular economy model, which focuses on taking existing products that would end up in landfills and putting them back into use. Levi Strauss is making various efforts on this front to repossess the products that consumers have finished with and find a way to use the materials in future production.

This model is great for the environment because rather than continuing to create apparel, it takes preexisting products and finds a way to give them value again. One such example is their Authorized Vintage collection. In a press release about the collection, Levi Strauss said, "The upcycling of these pre-worn pieces exemplifies conscious consumption and our commitment to long-term and sustainable manufacturing practices."

Another way Levi Strauss is committing to the circular

economy is with the recycling bins they have been placing in their storefronts in the United States and Canada. Rather than discarding old products, customers have the opportunity to recycle them so that the materials can be put into use again.

One of the challenges of Kelsey's position is convincing the people on the various teams within Levi Strauss that changing current practices to more sustainable ones is a worthy endeavor. It is not that the employees within the company do not want to embrace sustainability in every possible way. They just need to think strategically, considering the long-term health of the organization.

One effective way to convince coworkers of the need to switch practices is by looking at the financials. Kelsey and her team help to show the various departments within Levi Strauss how an investment in sustainability can be beneficial to the company's bottom line in the long run. Often sustainability practices require an investment in the present that will pay off over time because they help improve operation efficiencies.

One thing that makes her job a little easier is that the employees at Levi Strauss are committed to the values and mission of the company. They want to do good and help build a more sustainable brand. Therefore, helping to demonstrate the positive impact a particular switch can have on the environment or a community is an effective way to get people on board.

Additionally, Kelsey explained to me how patience and perseverance are essential to her position. Sometimes when she comes to a department with a new idea, it may be in a time of high stress. When this is the case, she realizes the timing may not be right and returns to the issue at a later date when implementation of a practice may be more feasible.

Kelsey's position also includes work with the marketing team. She does not work on the strategies or specific marketing tactics with the marketing department, but rather acts as a consultant on the incorporation of sustainability in their marketing materials. The marketing department works with people like Kelsey to make sure the claims they are making in are 100 percent accurate and portrayed in the best possible way.

She helps take complex sustainability concepts and break them down into chunks that are easily digestible for the consumers. She works with the marketing department to take data and facts that consumers would find too complex to really engage with and morph them into content that will resonate with consumers.

Additionally, she ensures that the company does not partake in the practice of greenwashing. While this practice is harmful for the sustainable fashion movement as a whole, it is also very risky for companies. Exposure for greenwashing is detrimental to a brand's image. No one likes to be tricked or deceived, so if consumers find out that a brand they are loyal to has been engaging in this practice, they will take their business elsewhere.

Another important aspect of sustainable marketing that Kelsey and I discussed was having the values of your brand align with sustainability. A brand solely focused on luxury fashion or sports performance with nothing in their mission statement or core values indicating a commitment to doing business responsibly that suddenly makes environmental claims can appear disingenuous to consumers. Brands need to be cautious of this and try to make sure that what their brand stands for is clear to consumers and aligns with social good if they plan to make claims regarding their sustainability practices.

Kelsey and I closed our conversation by discussing how Levi Strauss plans to further promote sustainable business moving forward. First and foremost, she elaborated by saying she wants to ensure that their sustainability practices reach 100 percent of their supply chain. It is not enough to just change one part of the operations; Levi Strauss wants to make a difference at every step of their product creation process.

Another program that Levi Strauss currently implements and will continue to invest in is their Worker Well-Being Program. The initiative was started in 2011 and works through Levi Strauss partnering with their suppliers and local organizations.

The focus of the program can vary depending on the needs and wants of the workers along the supply chain. Some of the different program focuses are financial empowerment, health and family well-being, and equality and acceptance.

In order to decide which of these programs to focus on, Levi Strauss has its suppliers survey their employees to determine what programs they would find most beneficial. After this process Levi Strauss works with local nonprofits and NGOs to implement them. On the Levi Strauss website, they talk about some of their targets for the future of the program.

By 2020 the company hopes to have 80 percent of its factories supported by the Worker Well-Being Program, which will in turn impact two hundred thousand workers. Another 2020 goal is to use 100 percent sustainable organic cotton in its production.

These initiatives are meant only to give an idea of some of Levi Strauss' goals in terms of sustainability moving forward and are in no way a full list of their commitment. Overall, it is clear that Levi Strauss is currently a leader in the space and intends to remain at the forefront of the movement.

In this chapter I highlight various macro level trends and initiatives that are key to the success of the sustainable fashion industry, but it is important to realize that all of these large-scale initiatives are only made possible through the commitment and hard work of individuals. The world needs people like Kelsey and the team at Levi Strauss to continue their passion and commitment to the cause in order to ensure its success.

CHAPTER 20

EFFECTS OF SUSTAINABILITY ON COMPANY CULTURE

One thing commonly overlooked by executives running a brand is the positive influence that incorporating sustainability within a company can have on the company culture. Incorporating sustainability within company culture not only builds authenticity and trust within a brand's consumer base but also helps to entice like-minded individuals to work for the company.

In my conversations with individuals within the sustainable fashion industry, I have been exposed to various companies that have greatly benefited from incorporating sustainability into their mission.

An example of sustainability changing the direction of a company is Alternative Apparel. In my conversation with the founder of Alternative Apparel, Evan Toporek, I learned how a company that is committed to doing good can have a positive influence on the company culture. Evan founded Alternative Apparel in 1995 as a company focused on providing its customers with quality embroidered shirts.

From this company stemmed the sub brand "Alternative Earth," founded in 2004. This sub line within the company grew more and more successful and over time became the focal point of the company. Evan decided to embrace this growing sub brand and have the entire brand move in the direction of becoming a company focused on sustainability.

He found that as the mission of his company shifted, the quality of those applying to join the organization increased greatly. He discovered that creative and talented people want to work for a company that is driven by more than just the bottom line.

In my conversation with Evan he remarked, "Alternative Apparel is not chasing a market opportunity, but rather sustainability is in their DNA." Additionally, he mentioned improvements in collaboration between employees when everyone is passionate about the mission of the company.

Another company founder I had the chance to speak with was Brian Linton, founder of United By Blue, which focuses on making "responsible durable products." One of their really interesting endeavors is their commitment to remove a pound of trash from the ocean for every product they sell. To date they have removed over a million pounds of trash from the ocean.

In our conversation he mentioned that having a company focused on a social mission makes it easier to have one unifying vision and goal for the company. It is easier to unite the employee base when everyone is passionate about the same thing. People are willing to work harder and go the extra mile when they are committed to something greater than themselves and even greater than the company they are working for.

He also touched on how the culture of focusing on sustainability can help a brand connect with their customer base. United By Blue organizes beach cleanups and often sees many of their customers come and volunteer with the employees of the company. Through apparel, United By Blue is able to unite likeminded and committed individuals so they can accomplish great things.

Another conversation I had where the impact of sustainability on a company culture was abundantly clear was with Paul Hendricks, an environmental responsibility manager at

Patagonia. I detail the conversation in a coming chapter, but I could not leave out some of what I learned from Paul in a chapter regarding sustainability and company culture. Paul detailed for me that a common understanding of Patagonia's overall mission involving a commitment to save the environment and do business in an ethical fashion is something that serves to unite the entire employee base. This recognition of working toward something larger than yourself can aid in collaboration.

An element of my conversation with Kelsey Pecherer cannot be left out either. Kelsey tries to see how sustainability can be strategically interwoven into the business model. She has a team of experts who stay up to date with the latest new information regarding sustainable practices. In doing this, she takes new sustainability practices and ideas and proposes them to various departments in the company that may be able to leverage them.

While she must do her job to convince them that it is a worthy endeavor, she said the company culture makes her job much easier than it would be in other organizations. Because people within Levi Strauss genuinely want to do good—and it is baked into their overall values and mission statement—weaving new sustainability practices into the business is that much more feasible.

Overall it has become clear to me that sustainability can help draw top level talent to an organization and unite employees in their efforts for change. By creating a culture that is so fueled by something bigger than oneself, the mindsets with which people approach their everyday work is wondrously transformed.

CHAPTER 21

WHAT SUSTAINABILITY MEANS AT PATAGONIA

———

There is possibly no brand more associated with the sustainable fashion movement than Patagonia, which has been at the forefront of the movement for the entirety of the brand's existence. Even their mission statement is focused solely on how their business can help preserve and protect our environment.

This statement reads: "Build the best product, cause no unnecessary harm, use business to inspire and implement solutions to the environmental crisis." Led by the legendary and inspirational Yvon Chouinard, the company maintains its values of simplicity and utility, which stem from the company's initial start by climbers and surfers.

All of the sports that Patagonia makes gear for—climbing, surfing, fly fishing, skiing, paddling, snowboarding, and trail running—are silent sports that enable us to fully connect with the nature surrounding us when we are engaging in them. The company's clear appreciation for nature motivates them to devote their time, services, and at least 1 percent of all sales to the environment's well-being.

To take a closer look at how sustainability works at Patagonia, I interviewed one of Patagonia's environmental responsibility managers, Paul Hendricks. In this conversion, I learned how an industry leader manages its sustainability platform and how its social mission factors into every aspect of the company's operations.

Sustainability at Patagonia is spearheaded by teams whose sole purpose is to look at Patagonia's impact as a global company, make sure they are minimizing environmental impact, and ensure they remain a top company from a social issues angle. These committed teams can be broken down further into internal sustainability operations and external teams that handle Patagonia's sustainability initiatives involving consumers, nonprofits, partnerships, etc.

Within the internal teams, some handle the social issues and some handle environmental issues. The team dealing with social issues audits and assesses Patagonia's labor practices by ensuring that the suppliers they use are fair trade certified, meaning that the employees of these suppliers receive a fair wage and enjoy safe working conditions.

The other half of the team handling internal sustainability issues at Patagonia looks at the footprint the brand itself is making. As a global company Patagonia realizes how widespread its impact can be and wants to ensure it prevents as much harm to the environment as it possibly can. To accomplish this, they take both their supply chain into account and their own company facilities.

In terms of their supply chain, they consider their energy use, water use, waste created, chemical pollution, and the impact of transporting their goods. Additionally, they look at the impact their operations at headquarters and retail storefronts around the country have on the environment.

The other side of the sustainability initiative at Patagonia is the team that deals with external affairs. One of the things this external sustainability team handles is their 1 percent For the Planet initiative. In this global movement started by Patagonia, companies agree to donate 1 percent of all sales to support environmental organizations by providing funding at the grassroots level.

This initiative has already donated 175 million dollars toward protecting the planet. The team at Patagonia dedicated to this initiative searches for some of the best environmental organizations and helps provide them with funding to keep making a difference. This team also helps to manage other corporate partnerships like their partnerships with B Corp, Sustainable Apparel Coalition, and the Fair Labor Association to name a few.

The commitment to sustainability does not end with the teams specified to work on this initiative. Sustainability is a consideration for every dimension of the company. From the finance department to the marketing department, sustainability is always a part of the conversation. Paul Hendricks explained that for a company to really be sustainable it needs an awareness and commitment from everyone within the organization.

For example, the work of the sales forecasting team is pivotal to Patagonia's reduction of its overall environmental impact because if they miscalculate their expected sales, Patagonia will be left with thousands of unpurchased products, which causes a great deal of waste.

The commitment to do the least harm possible in business operations is made evident from the very beginning of every employee's career at Patagonia. Paul elaborated, "Part of the onboarding process is realizing that you are here to use business as an agent for change."

Paul made it clear that being a sustainable brand is an ongoing commitment. At Patagonia they are constantly searching for new and innovative ways to reduce their impact, whether that be utilizing a new technology or conducting experiments to find more eco-friendly textiles to use in the creation of their products.

One important thing to remember about Patagonia is that while they pride themselves on sustainability, they do not cast aside the importance of profits. They understand that by maintaining profitability they are increasing the scale and resources with which they can move forth and make the biggest and best possible impact.

Patagonia CEO Rose Marcario said the following: "People identify with the care of the environment. We've got to take care of our nest. People recognize Patagonia as a company that's going to keep asking deep questions about our supply chain, the impact we're having in the world, and looking at business through a more holistic lens other than profit. Profit is important; if it wasn't, you wouldn't be talking to me. But profit isn't the only measure of success."

With sustainability so deeply interwoven within company culture and a clear commitment to continuous improvement, Patagonia will continue to spearhead the sustainable fashion movement. Their commitment will continue to set the example of embracing sustainability for other companies.

CHAPTER 22

POLITICAL ACTIVISM IN APPAREL

———

Much of my research and exploration of the fashion industry has revolved around what companies are doing and can do to embrace sustainability in their operations. However, some companies are extending their impact in a positive way beyond just their own operations. These companies have begun to leverage their power as global brands to be agents for change.

Large companies can be agents for change for a few reasons. One is resources; large global brands have key resources like money and many employees at their disposal. However, perhaps one of the most tremendous abilities large companies have is their ability to reach millions of people through their marketing messages. Global brands can reach people with their marketing materials due to their large and loyal customer base.

One of the best examples of a company leveraging their position as a global brand is yup, you guessed it—Patagonia. Patagonia has not shied away from speaking their mind on politics when it comes to saving the environment. Patagonia has always been politically active but in recent months has increased their activism even more to fight against some of the actions being taken by the Trump administration.

Patagonia CEO, Rose Marcario, commented, "It's built into our mission statement to use business to inspire and implement solutions to the environmental crisis." It makes sense then that a company who sees saving the environment as part of their purpose would take action when the government enacts legislation that is counter to environmental protection.

One way Patagonia engaged in politics was during the 2016 election cycle. They launched an initiative called "Vote Our Planet" where they encouraged consumers to take action to protect our planet by exercising their right to vote. In their messaging, they voiced what many people felt—the desire to boycott the entire election process because of frustrations with corruption within the political system.

After acknowledging the frustration many were dealing with, they emphasized the importance of still voting for candidates who will help to protect our environment. Their company website featured various resources for consumers to educate themselves on the stances being taken by politicians regarding the environment. They provided a link to help people find their closest voting location and even gave all their employees election day off so they could get out and vote.

The intent and mission of their campaign is summed up with some words from a statement released by Rose Marcario. "We must keep fighting—whether we're putting points on the board, or playing defense—against the endless forces willing to trade the long-term health of our planet for short-term profit. We must counter and overpower those forces with sustained, energetic and strategic activism."

While election day may not have ended with the result Patagonia wanted, they have not been discouraged and continue to fight. Most recently Patagonia has taken up an initiative to fight back against the Trump administration's reduction of public lands. The Trump administration is trying to reduce Bears Ears and Grand Staircase-Escalante National Monuments by nearly two million acres.

Patagonia founder Yvon Chouinard has been extremely outspoken regarding the issue and has stated that he plans to sue the administration for what Patagonia claims is an illegal move by the government. In efforts to save the land, Patagonia has also worked to uncover the true motives behind the move to reduce the public lands.

In an article titled "It Was Always about the Oil, Coal, Gas, and Uranium," author Lisa Pike Sheehy gives some background about why the president wants to reduce these public lands. The cause and effect detailed in the article is that large companies who spend millions of dollars lobbying the government want these lands to become private so they can extract the significant energy resources located in these lands. The figures regarding how much of these energy resources are located in the lands Trump is attempting to take away from the public are as follows: 11.4 billion tons of coal, 500,000 tons of uranium, and 90,000 acres of land containing oil and gas. These figures help shed light on the real motives behind the Trump's administration attempt to peel back public lands.

Patagonia is not alone in this initiative to fight for public lands. Outdoor apparel company REI took a stance against Trump's actions as well. They released a corporate statement detailing their concerns and even included a policy analysis. They questioned the short four-month review of public lands and claimed that the government's actions are in violation of the Antiquities Act. Besides REI and Patagonia, brands North Face and Arc'teryx took a political stance with their donations to organizations committed to protecting public lands.

To add my own personal account of my experience with Patagonia, I have found that their political activism has increased both my engagement and loyalty with the company. When I see the alert pop up on my phone that I have an email from Patagonia, I am far more likely to open it than any other emails I receive from retailers.

Unlike traditional retailers, when I receive an email from them, I am eager to see what new innovation they have incorporated into their product development or new political initiative they are engaged in. Most retailers are often just pushing products with discounts and new product offerings, but Patagonia is not. Their varied messaging keeps me engaged with their marketing materials and builds my loyalty to the brand.

My loyalty is heightened because I can see firsthand that the money I spend with them is helping to make a positive impact and enact change within the industry. I think my own experiences are probably similar to what other socially conscious consumers must feel.

Clearly, companies can use their resources and global recognition to do more than just focus on profits. They can use their stage to not only enact change, but also stand up and fight against policies that do not align with their company's values.

I want to close this chapter on political activism with a quote from one of the greatest activists around, Yvon Chouinard. Yvon said the following regarding activism: "People may be afraid of the term 'activist' because they associate it with eco-sabotage and violent protests, but I'm talking about normal citizens who want the government to live up to its obligations to protect our air, water and all other natural resources. Activists have an infectious passion about the issues they support, whether they are mothers fighting to clean up toxic landfills that are killing their children or farmers trying to hold on to their fourth-generation family business threatened by urban sprawl. These are the people on the front lines, trying either to make the government obey its own laws or to recognize the need for a new law."

CHAPTER 23

EMPOWERMENT X SSEKO

———

This stop is a pretty spectacular one. On my original trip through the fashion industry, I discovered this stop while making a different one (exploring sustainable footwear). But as I learned more and more about Sseko Designs, an ethical fashion brand based out of Uganda, I knew we had to make this its very own stop. So get ready because while this was a late edition to our trip, often those are the best ones.

Sseko Designs is built around the idea of creating a community where women can empower each other through a self-sustaining business model. This idea is the essence of sustainable fashion. While many, many fashion companies are abusing their labor force with unfair wages and dangerous working conditions, Sseko is not only providing these things but taking it even a step further and providing opportunity for these women.

The clearest way for me to walk through the impact this company is having on society is to walk you through the core issues and solutions as outlined by the team at Sseko themselves.

Issue #1—Female students in Uganda cannot pursue higher education that would allow them to rise to leadership positions in their communities because of a lack of economic opportunity.

The Sseko Solution: Sseko employs high-achieving recent women high school graduates for nine months. This period is during the gap between high school and the start of university. Half of their salary from each month goes into a savings account that can only be accessed for tuition. This is done to not only ensure that the money goes toward school but to help these young women avoid the great social pressures they feel to use their money for their families. At the end of their time working, Sseko Designs matches 100 percent of the funds the women have saved through grants.

Issue #2—In male dominated societies like Uganda, women are not afforded the same employment opportunities that men are.

The Sseko Solution: In order to counter this male dominant society, Sseko provides employment opportunities to women who are too old to return to the education system. They partner with a nonprofit to provide work with fair wages and safe conditions to women who have recently exited the commercial sex industry.

Issue #3—Although charities and nonprofits are essential to helping society in some situations, they can also play a negative role by creating dependencies and hurting the local economy.

The Sseko Solution: With this idea in mind, Sseko powers their solutions largely through the business sector. They have created a sustainable and self-sufficient business model that capitalizes on the idea of conscious consumerism.

Issue #4—Women all over the world struggle to find meaningful work that they can support themselves and their families with.

The Sseko Solution: Through the Sseko Fellowship Program, Sseko Designs is giving women in the United States the opportunity to launch their own social enterprise by selling Sseko products. This provides these women with meaningful work and builds a community where women can work together to empower each other.

Pretty powerful stuff right there. If you were curious about how the program was working out—I mean, how could you not be—Sseko is sending their 106th woman to college this year.

I thought this would really be the perfect way for us to close out our stop to explore the idea that change is possible. You do not have to take my word for it—just ask the incredible team at Sseko Designs.

CONCLUSION

———

Well, this is the end of our trip together. Thanks for taking the trip with me and congratulations for making it all the way to the end!

Like the end of any good trip, we can now take some time to look back and reflect on where we have been and what we have learned along the way. Think of this as us sitting back at home and looking through all the pictures we took—reminiscing on our journey together. This last stop on our journey is important to help us remember all the things we have learned.

* * *

Stop #1—Industry Analysis

Where did it all begin again? Oh that's right… with the Pulse Report. One of the major takeaways from our journey is that this report is a go-to resource for anyone who is serious about understanding the sustainable fashion space. This report provided us with solid summary statistics of the industry, detailed projections for its growth and what effects this would have on the world. It even gave us a useful metric to understand the impact of each stage of a fashion product's life cycle with the Pulse Score. Wow! That sure was a great start to our time together. After that we touched on some of the main drivers of the sustainable fashion movement, like the sharing economy and changing consumer mindsets.

Stop #2—Why We Need Change

Next up was gaining our understanding of why we need change in the industry. We started out with some emotional stories—like Alejandra Carrero's life-changing trip to a factory in China. Then we explored why fashion brands should seek sustainable practices, not just because it is the right thing to do but also because their long-term success depends on it.

Then on to clearing up a common misconception in the industry and getting our facts straight. Finally, we closed this stop off with the tragic story of the factory collapse in Bangladesh.

Stop #3—How Change Can Happen

Once we fully grasped the necessity of change in this industry, we moved on to explore how this change can happen. We began this stop by looking at the idea of community building, which is one of the most important factors in the success of this movement. By uniting the efforts of individuals, businesses, organizations, and governments, we will see real change in fashion.

This community building can come in a multitude of ways such as events, blogs, and company initiatives. One of my favorite stops in this section was when we got to explore the seemingly endless amount of innovation occurring in the space. There are innovation challenges, new materials being discovered for textiles, new ways to approach data analysis, and companies totally recreating business models.

We also examined topics like what influence celebrities can have and how we can best leverage what we know about psychology to help propel sustainable fashion forward. We closed this stop off with an in-depth look at apparel rental and how important this new business model is to society becoming more sustainable.

Stop #4—Change Is Possible

After all of that amazing journeying we ended here—looking at examples of why change is possible. First we looked at companies, like Nike, that had successfully shifted to make sustainability a priority. Then we took one last look at the Pulse Report to see what kind of actionable steps companies of all sizes can take, at each and every step of their value chain.

Then we revisited the tragic story of Bangladesh to see what kind of change this devastating incident caused within the industry. Following this we took an in-depth look at two powerhouses in the sustainable fashion world—Patagonia and Levi Strauss & Co. Finally, we closed with a beautiful story about the work at a company called Sseko Designs.

The main takeaway from this last stop is that there is hope. The fashion industry is changing and can continue to change. We do not have to sit back and wait and hope that it changes. As we learned on our journey, one individual has the power to make a huge difference.

You do not have to go out and start your own organization or company. We still have the power to help enact this change. We can change how we consume goods, make smarter buying decisions to support brands that are doing the right thing, and most importantly help spread this awareness.

Spreading awareness of this issue is hands down one of the best things we can do to help make the fashion industry more sustainable. This issue is still not nearly well known enough in society today and you have the power to begin changing that.

* * *

While this may be the end of our trip together, this does not have to be the end of your exploration of this dynamic industry. Countless websites, books, articles, etc. can aid you in further understanding this revolutionary movement of sustainable fashion.

I hope you enjoyed yourself and learned a thing or two along the way.

SOURCES

----

*Note – sources appear by chapter in the order they appear

Chapter 1

"Pulse of the Fashion Industry." *Global Fashion Agenda & The Boston Consulting Group*, 2017.

http://globalfashionagenda.com/wp-content/uploads/2017/05/Pulse-of-the-Fashion-Industry_2017.pdf.

Chapter 2

Todeschini, Bruna Villa, Marcelo Nogueira Cortimiglia, Daniela Callegaro-de-Menezes, and Antonio Ghezzi. "Innovative and sustainable business models in the fashion industry: Entrepreneurial drivers, opportunities, and challenges" *Business Horizons*, 2017. Volume 60, Issue 6, Pages 759-770,

http://www.sciencedirect.com/science/article/pii/S0007681317301015.

D'Souza, Annie. "8 Fashion Brands That Use

Recycled Materials." *Brit + Co*, Brit + Co, 14 Dec. 2014,

www.brit.co/recycled-fashion-designers/.

Chapter 4

Mellery-Pratt, Robin. "5 Sustainability Threats

Facing Fashion." *BoF*, The Business of Fashion, 2018.

https://www.businessoffashion.com/articles/intelligence/5-sustain-ability-threats-facing-fashion.

Spear, Stefanie. "10 Most Profound Passages

From 'Let My People Go Surfing.'" *EcoWatch*, EcoWatch, 19 Sept. 2016,

www.ecowatch.com/let-my-people-go-surfing-2008599492.html.

Chapter 5

Wicker, Alden. "We Have No Idea How Bad Fashion Actually Is for the Environment." *Racked*, Racked, 15 Mar. 2017,

www.racked.com/2017/3/15/14842476/fashion-climate-change-environment-pollution.

Wicker, Alden. "Fashion Is the 8th Most Polluting Industry?" *Ecocult*, Ecocult, May 2018,

ecocult.com/now-know-fashion-5th-polluting-industry-equal-livestock

Drew, Deborah, and Genevieve Yehounme. "The Apparel Industry's Environmental Impact in 6 Graphics." *Shifting to Renewable Energy Can Save U.S.*

Consumers Money | World Resources Institute, 5 July 2017,

www.wri.org/blog/2017/07/apparel-industrys-environmental-impact-6-graphics.

Chapter 6

Yardley, Jim. "Report on Bangladesh Building Collapse Finds Wide-

spread Blame." *The New York Times*, The New York Times, 22
May 2013,

www.nytimes.com/2013/05/23/world/asia/report-on-bangladesh-
building-collapse-finds-widespread-blame.html.

Chapter 7

"Hope for Environmental Activists: Patagonia CEO Rose Marcario
Shares Why She's Optimistic About the Future." *B The Change*,
B The Change, 23 Nov. 2016,

bthechange.com/hope-for-environmental-activists-pata-
gonia-ceo-rose-marcario-shares-why-shes-optimis-
tic-about-the-5edece19e96f.

Chapter 8

"Our Origins." *Sustainable Apparel Coalition*, Sustainable Apparel
Coalition, 2018,

apparelcoalition.org/origins/.

"Why Fair Trade—Why Buy Fair Trade." *Fair Trade Certified*, Fair
Trade USA, 2018, www.fairtradecertified.org/why-fair-trade.

"About B Corps." *Tillak | Certified B Corporation*, B Lab, 2018, bcorporation.net/about-b-corps.

"Do Fashion Better." *Common Objective*, Ethical Fashion Group Ltd, 2018, www.commonobjective.co/

"About The Ellen MacArthur Foundation." *Ellen MacArthur Foundation*, Ellen MacArthur Foundation, 2017, www.ellenmacarthurfoundation.org/about.

Birkner, Cherie. "Kate Black // Founder of EcoSessions // Blogger & Author of Magnifeco." *Sustainable Fashion Matterz*, 2017,

www.sustainablefashionmatterz.com/blog/kate-black-ecosessions-magnifeco.

Chapter 9

"Nike Design With Grind Challenge." *Participate In Creating Social Impact—OpenIDEO*, OpenIDEO, 2018,

www.openideo.com/challenge-briefs/nike-design-with-grind.

"Nike Circular Innovation Challenge." *NIKE GRIND*, Nike, Inc., 2018, www.nikeinnovationchallenge.com/.

"Nike Seeks Material Recovery, Design Ideas with 'Limitless Potential.'" *Sustainablebrands.com*, Sustainable Life Media Inc., 2018,

www.sustainablebrands.com/news_and_views/next_economy/
sustainable_brands/nike_challenge_material_recovery_product_design.

"Nike Material Recovery Challenge." *Ninesights*, NineSigma Holdings Inc., 2018,

ninesights.ninesigma.com/servlet/hype/IMT?userAction=Browse.

"The Higg Index—Sustainable Apparel Coalition." *Sustainable Apparel Coalition*, Sustainable Apparel Coalition, 2018, apparelcoalition.org/the-higg-index/.

"The SAC—Sustainable Apparel Coalition." *Sustainable Apparel Coalition*, Sustainable Apparel Coalition, 2018,

apparelcoalition.org/the-sac/.

"What Is an EP&L?" *Kering*,

Kering, 2017, www.kering.com/en/sustainability/whatisepl.

Preuss, Simone. "6 Sustainable Textile Innovations That Will Change the Fashion Industry." *Fashionunited*, Fashionunited, 9 Oct. 2017, fashionunited.com/news/business/6-sustainable-textile-innova-tions-that-will-change-the-fashion-industry/2017100917734.

D'Souza, Annie. "8 Fashion Brands That Use Recycled Materials." *Brit + Co*, Brit + Co, 14 Dec. 2014,

www.brit.co/recycled-fashion-designers/.

"What Is Upcycling?" *Looptworks*, Looptworks, 2018, www. looptworks.com/pages/what-is-upcycling.

Bobila, Maria. "5 Up-and-Coming Brands Dedicated to Reworking Vintage Materials." *Fashionista*, Breaking Media, Inc., 10 May 2016,

fashionista.com/2016/05/upcycle-vintage-fashion-brands.

Bauck, Whitney. "How Technology Is Shaping the Future of Sustain-able Fashion." *Fashionista*, Breaking Media, Inc., 23 Oct. 2017,

fashionista.com/2017/10/fashion-design-technology-sustainable-tex-tiles-2017.

"Natsai Audrey Chieza." *Natsai Audrey Chieza*, 2018, www.natsa-iaudrey.co.uk/.

Chapter 10

Global Change Award, H&M Foundation, 2017,

globalchangeaward.com/about-the-award/.

"Global Change Award Fashion Innovation Challenge." *Accenture*, Accenture, 2018,

www.accenture.com/us-en/event-global-change-award.

Chapter 11

"13 Ethical & Sustainable Shoe Brands We're Loving." *The Green Hub*, Green Hub Online, 4 June 2018, thegreenhubonline. com/2018/02/22/13-ethical-sustainable-shoe-brands-were-loving/.

"Our Story." *Allbirds*, Allbirds, Inc., 2018, www.allbirds.com/pages/our-story.

Drummond, Jack. "Meet Veja, the World's Most Ethical Sneaker Brand." *Highsnobiety*, Titel Media GMBH, 9 Aug. 2016, www. highsnobiety.com/2015/09/16/sebastien-kopp-francois-morillion-veja-interview/.

Chapter 12

"5 Celebrities Who Are Behind The Shift To Sustainable Fashion." *Marie Claire* , Marie Claire, 31 July 2017,

www.marieclaire.co.za/fashion/celebs-who-support-the-sustainable-fashion-movement.

DuFault, Amy. "Emma Watson and Will.i.am Back Sustainable Fashion." *The Guardian*, Guardian News and Media, 3 Oct. 2014,

www.theguardian.com/sustainable-business/sustainable-fashion-blog/2014/oct/03/10-celebrities-backing-sustainable-fashion.

Klara, Robert. "How Beats Used Celeb Marketing to Become Millennials' Favorite Audio Brand." *Adweek*, Adweek, 3 Jan. 2017,

www.adweek.com/brand-marketing/how-beats-used-celeb-marketing-become-millennials-favorite-audio-brand-175314/.

"Most Followed Accounts on Twitter 2018." *Statista*, 2018,

www.statista.com/statistics/273172/twitter-accounts-with-the-most-followers-worldwide/.

Pustetto, Megan. "8 Eco-Friendly Celebrities You Should Know—

The Trend Spotter." *Fashion Trends and Style Blog*, 12 Oct. 2017, www.thetrendspotter.net/8-eco-friendly-celebrities/.

Chapter 13

Manning, Christie. *The Psychology of Sustainable Behavior.*

Minnesota Pollution Control Agency, Sept. 2009,

www.pca.state.mn.us/sites/default/files/p-ee1-01.pdf.

Miller, Hannah. "Getting behind the Psychology of Sustainability."

GreenBiz, GreenBiz Group Inc., 28 Feb. 2013, www.greenbiz.com/news/2013/02/28/getting-behind-psychology-sustainability.

Sethi, Simran. "Green Brain." *Simra Sethi*, 3 July 2017, simransethi.com/the-green-brain/.

Chapter 14

Omotoso, Moni. "Fast Fashion vs the Slow Fashion Movement." *UTELIER*,

1 Mar. 2017, insider.utelier.com/features/uthink/fast-fashion-vs-slow-fashion/.

Pookulangara, Sanjukta, and Arlesa Shephard . "Slow Fashion Movement: Understanding Consumer Perceptions—An Exploratory Study." *Elsevier,*

Journal of Retailing and Consumer Services,

file:///C:/Users/TylerSlow%20fashion%20movement-%20Understanding%20consumer%20perception.pdf.

Chapter 15

Bain, Marc. "Can Rent the Runway Ever Become the Spotify of Fashion?" *Quartz,* Quartz, 18 Oct. 2017, qz.com/1104344/can-rent-the-runway-ever-become-the-spotify-of-fashion/.

"DEEP DIVE: Millennial Lifestyles Drive Growth in Apparel Rental."

Coresight Research,

www.fungglobalretailtech.com/research/deep-dive-millennial-lifestyles-drive-growth-apparel-rental/.

"From Bags to Dresses, Fashion's Most Noteworthy Emerging Trend Is Renting." *The Fashion Law,* Nov. 2017,

www.thefashionlaw.com/home/from-bags-to-dresses-fashions-most-noteworthy-emerging-trend-is-renting.

Chapter 16

"Just Fix It: How Nike Learned to Embrace Sustainability." *BoF*, The Business of Fashion, 1 Nov. 2016, www.businessoffashion.com/articles/people/just-fix-it-hannah-jones-nike.

Albanese, Maya. "How She Leads: Hannah Jones of Nike." *GreenBiz*, GreenBiz Group Inc., 6 Feb. 2012, www.greenbiz.com/blog/2012/02/06/how-she-leads-hannah-jones-nike.

Farra, Emily. "Mara Hoffman on Her New Sustainable Business-And Changing Her Label's Look." *Vogue*, Vogue, 26 May 2017, www.vogue.com/article/mara-hoffman-new-sustainable-fashion-business-natural-fabrics.

"Innovation Quotes." *BrainyQuote*, Xplore, 2018, www.brainyquote.com/topics/innovation.

Chapter 17

"Pulse of the Fashion Industry." *Global Fashion Agenda & The Boston Consulting Group*, 2017.

http://globalfashionagenda.com/wp-content/uploads/2017/05/Pulse-of-the-Fashion-Industry_2017.pdf.

Chapter 18

Nittle, Nadra. "After the Rana Plaza Collapse, Are Garment Workers Any Safer?" *Racked*, Vox Media, Inc., 13 Apr. 2018,

www.racked.com/2018/4/13/17230770/rana-plaza-collapse-anniversary-garment-workers-safety.

"About the Accord." *The Bangladesh Accord*, Accord on Fire and Safety in Bandladesh, 2017, bangladeshaccord.org/about/.

Westerman, Ashley. "4 Years After Rana Plaza Tragedy, What's Changed For Bangladeshi Garment Workers?" *NPR*, NPR, 30 Apr. 2017,

www.npr.org/sections/parallels/2017/04/30/525858799/4-years-after-rana-plaza-tragedy-whats-changed-for-bangladeshi-garment-workers.

"About the Alliance for Bangladesh Worker Safety." *Alliance for Bangladesh Worker Safety*, Alliance for Bangladesh Worker Safety, 2018,

www.bangladeshworkersafety.org/who-we-are/about-the-alliance.

Chapter 19

"A Vintage Homecoming: Introducing Levi's®

Authorized Vintage." *Levi Strauss*, Levi Strauss & Co., 9 Nov. 2017,
www.levistrauss.com/unzipped-blog/2017/11/10/vintage-home-
coming-introducing-levis-authorized-vintage/.

"Worker Well-Being." *Levi Strauss*, Levi Strauss & Co., 2018, www.
levistrauss.com/sustainability/people/apparel-workers/.

Chapter 20

None

Chapter 21

"Patagonia's Mission Statement." *Patagonia*,

Patagonia, 2018, www.patagonia.com/company-info.html.

Chua, Jasmin Malik. "Patagonia CEO Rose Marcario: 'Profit Isn't
the Only Measure of Success.'" *Ecouterre*,

Internet Brands, Inc., 21 Nov. 2014,

inhabitat.com/ecouterre/patagonia-ceo-rose-marcario-profit-isnt-the-only-measure-of-success/.

Chapter 22

"4 Companies Getting Politically Active—and Growing." *The Mission Daily*, A Medium Corporation, 21 Feb. 2018,

medium.com/the-mission/4-companies-getting-politically-active-and-growing-710125aeed99.

"It Was Always About Oil, Coal, Gas and Uranium." *The Cleanest Line*, Patagonia, 29 May 2018,

www.patagonia.com/blog/2018/03/it-was-always-about-oil-coal-gas-and-uranium.

Pinsker, Joe. "Patagonia, REI, and the Politics of 'The President Stole Your Land.'" *The Atlantic*, Atlantic Media Company,

5 Dec. 2017, www.theatlantic.com/business/archive/2017/12/patagonia-rei-bears-ears-president-stole/547577/.

Spear, Stefanie. "10 Most Profound Passages From 'Let My People Go Surfing.'" *EcoWatch*, EcoWatch, 19 Sept. 2016,

www.ecowatch.com/let-my-people-go-surfing-2008599492.html.

Chapter 23

"Mission & Impact." *Sseko Designs*, Sseko Designs,

2018, ssekodesigns.com/mission-and-impact/.

ACKNOWLEDGEMENTS

———

There are countless people I want to thank for making this possible. First, I want to thank all of the amazing individuals who took the time to have a conversation with me about a topic we both feel so passionately about. I want to thank Eric Koester and his team for making this all possible with their innovative approach to learning and help along the way. I want to thank Michaela McCool for being my sounding board and support system. And finally, I want to thank my parents who inspire me every day with their work ethic and love for our family. Thanks for all the opportunities you have given me—this would have never been possible without you.

Made in the USA
Lexington, KY
06 September 2019